The Absent Father Effect on Daughters

Understand the Impact of Growing up Without a Father, Overcome the Legacy of Father Neglect, and Heal Father Wounds

Chloe Vaughn

Contents

Introduction

As a young girl, I remember longing for my father's presence in my life. The empty seat at the dinner table, the silence where a comforting voice should have been, the missing cheers from the sidelines at my school events, and the absence of a protective presence when I faced my first heartbreak were the constant reminders of a void that shaped my world. If you, too, have grown up without a father, you understand the profound impact this void can have on a daughter's heart and psyche.

In the pages of this book, I welcome you to explore the effect of having an absent father and begin to understand, heal, and recover. Together, we will explore the complex emotions and challenges of growing up without a father's presence, guidance, love, and support. Whether you are the daughter of a single mother or your father was physically present but emotionally absent, the scars of this experience can run deep.

As an adult, you may grapple with feelings of abandonment, struggle with self-worth, or find yourself repeatedly in unhealthy relationships. You might question your own lovability or find it challenging to trust others fully. These are the invisible wounds that many daughters of absent fathers carry with them into adulthood.

But here's the truth: You are not alone, and your pain is valid. Through this book, I want to create a safe space where you can acknowledge your experiences, validate your emotions, and begin the process of healing. By sharing personal stories, insights from experts, and practical strategies for growth, I hope to give you a sense of wholeness.

We'll examine the psychological impact of a father's absence on a daughter's development, exploring how it can shape one's sense of identity, self-esteem, and attachment patterns. We'll also look at how these early experiences can influence relationships, both romantic and platonic, and discuss tools for building healthier connections.

Throughout the book, you'll find a blend of personal anecdotes, research-backed insights, and therapeutic techniques designed to help you process your emotions, reframe your narratives, and cultivate resilience. Whether you're seeking to understand your past, improve your present, or build a brighter future, this book is written to be a compassionate companion on your path.

As someone who has walked this road myself, I understand the courage it takes to confront the pain of an absent father. I've struggled with the questions, the doubts, and the longing for answers. But I've also discovered the incredible strength and resilience within each of us. My goal is to help you tap into that inner power and reclaim your story.

Whether you're picking up this book for the first time or returning to it as a source of support, know that you are worthy of love, healing, and happiness. Your father's absence is not a reflection on you. It does not define you, and his choices do not determine your value. You have the power to rewrite your narrative and create a life filled with joy, purpose, and fulfilling relationships.

You are not defined by your father's absence or the legacy it has left you. Your resilience, courage, and boundless potential define you.

Chapter 1

There was a moment during a school play when the auditorium lights dimmed, and the audience fell silent in anticipation. Standing on the stage, I scanned the crowd, my eyes moving from one proud father to the next, dads beaming, clapping, and whispering words of encouragement to their children. But mine was never there. The emptiness hit me like a weight in my chest, a silent reminder of the father who had always been absent. The absence of a father in a daughter's life is not just a missing figure in the audience; it is an emotional and psychological void that shapes her in ways both seen and unseen. This chapter explores the profound impact of "Fatherless Daughter Syndrome," a term that encapsulates the unique struggles of growing up without a steady paternal presence. From the lifelong search for validation to the emotional complexities that arise from this absence, understanding these effects is the first step toward healing.

The Emotional Void Left Behind

The absence of a father often creates an emotional void that can linger like a shadow, subtly influencing a daughter's life in ways both seen and unseen. This void manifests in a constant search for approval, a yearning for the affirmation and acceptance that might have come naturally from a father's love. There's an underlying sense of incompleteness, a nagging feeling of not being entirely whole or worthy, which can erode self-esteem and self-worth. This longing for paternal guidance and protection can leave you vulnerable, leading to either emotional numbness or a heightened sensitivity to rejection and criticism. You might oscillate between these extremes, struggling to find a balance that feels right.

This absence can stifle emotional growth, making forming and maintaining healthy emotional connections challenging. You might find it difficult to open up or trust others, fearing they, too, might leave or disappoint you. This can lead to emotional suppression, where feelings are bottled up, or an inclination toward self-blame or guilt, as though you are somehow responsible for the absence or its impact on your life. These emotional hurdles can hinder your ability to process and express emotions healthily, creating a cycle of isolation and loneliness.

The link between the father's absence and self-esteem issues is significant. This often results in relentless self-criticism and an internalized belief of being unlovable. This can manifest as a harsh inner voice that questions your worth and abilities, making it difficult to accept yourself fully. You might find yourself striving for perfection, using overachievement to prove your value to yourself and others. This need for validation can also extend into relationships, where you seek approval and affirmation from partners or friends, hoping to fill the void left by your father.

To cope with these feelings, you may adopt maladaptive strategies that, while offering temporary relief, can ultimately be detrimental. Overachievement can become a double-edged sword, where success is pursued at the expense of personal well-being. Alternatively, you might seek validation through relationships, placing undue pressure on partners to fulfill unmet emotional needs during childhood. Emotional withdrawal from peers can also occur, as isolation feels safer than the risk of further rejection or disappointment.

Exploring Your Emotional Landscape

Take a moment to reflect on how the absence of a father has shaped your emotional landscape. Consider the following questions:

- In what ways have you sought approval or validation in your life?

- How do you perceive your self-worth, and what factors influence it?

- What coping mechanisms have you developed to manage your emotions?

- Do you lack self-confidence and feel insecure?

- Would you prefer to be in a romantic relationship with a man, even if the relationship is unhealthy?

Please take some time to think about these questions. By giving them deep consideration, you can uncover the patterns and beliefs that your father's absence has influenced. This self-awareness is an important step towards healing, allowing you to identify areas where change is needed and empowering you to seek healthier ways of relating to yourself and others. Recognizing these patterns is not about blaming yourself or your father; it's about understanding the impact of his absence and taking proactive steps to address it.

Coping with the Silent Impact

The absence of a father influences life in subtle, often unnoticed ways, shaping daily interactions and decisions. It lingers in the background, quietly affecting how you approach relationships, self-worth, and confidence. This silent impact extends into decision-making, where you might find yourself second-guessing choices, plagued by the fear of making a wrong move. The influence of an absent father can also create a persistent sense of unease, especially in social settings where others' fathers are present, serving as a constant reminder of what is missing in your own life. This underlying anxiety can leave you feeling out of place or uncertain in situations that seem effortless for others.

Moreover, the absence of a father can unconsciously affect how you view male relationships, often skewing your perceptions and expectations. You may unknowingly model these relationships on what you imagine a father-daughter dynamic should be based on cultural narratives or the relationships you observe around you. This modeling can lead to unrealistic expectations or misunderstandings, where you seek qualities in male figures that a fatherly presence should have fulfilled. On the other hand, you might find yourself drawn to men who are less accomplished or dependable because, deep down, you don't feel worthy of a man's love due to the wounds left by your father's abandonment. These influences, subtle yet profound, guide your interactions in ways you may not fully comprehend until you pause to reflect on them.

Behaviorally, these silent impacts may manifest in ways that are not immediately apparent to you. Indecisiveness can become a recurring theme, a hesitance to commit to choices for fear of unforeseen consequences. You may find yourself avoiding conflict or confrontation, preferring the path of least resistance to maintain harmony and avoid the discomfort associated with disagreements. This avoidance can stem from wanting to be accepted, not rock the boat, and maintaining a semblance of stability in a world that already feels uncertain without a fatherly anchor.

Societal expectations further compound these silent impacts, often reinforcing internalized beliefs about gender roles and the significance of paternal presence. There is a pervasive pressure to conform to traditional family structures, where the presence of a father is seen as the norm, and deviations from this are met with scrutiny or pity. As a result, you might feel the weight of stigma surrounding single-parent families, which can lead to feelings of inadequacy or shame. These societal pressures subtly influence your self-perception, pushing you to fit into molds that may not align with your authentic self.

In recognizing these silent impacts, seeking validation becomes a vital step in the healing process. Acknowledging how the absence of a father has shaped your experiences allows you to take ownership of your narrative, understanding that these influences are not a reflection of your worth but rather the circumstances you've been dealt. Finding supportive networks, whether through participation in support groups or engaging with narratives of similar experiences, offers a sense of community and understanding. These spaces provide the validation and empathy needed to unravel the complexities of growing up without a father, offering a platform for sharing stories and learning from others who have walked a similar path.

Understanding Silent Influences

Consider the following questions as you reflect on the silent impacts of your father's absence:

- How do societal expectations around family structures influence your perception of your own family dynamics?

- In what ways have you modeled relationships based on what you imagine a father-daughter dynamic should be?

- How does the absence of a father influence your decision-making and interactions in social settings?

- How has not having a father directly impacted the type of men you have romantic relationships with?

- In your professional life, do you find it hard to stand up for yourself with male colleagues?

Reflecting on these questions can help you identify the subtle ways in which your father's absence has shaped your life. By understanding these influences, you gain the power to make conscious choices to free yourself from the silent impacts that have guided you thus far.

The Ripple Effect on Identity

Growing up without a father can make understanding yourself more challenging. A father often plays a key role in shaping a child's sense of identity, guiding values, behavior, and self-worth. Without that influence, you might find yourself searching for a sense of stability and direction. The absence of a paternal role model can bring up questions about who you are and who you want to become, sometimes leading to uncertainty in areas like personal boundaries, self-esteem, confidence, and gender roles. You may struggle to define what it means to be a woman or an individual without a father's presence, leaving parts of your identity unsettled or incomplete.

Societal norms and expectations can further complicate this internal struggle, pressing the weight of traditional roles and familial structures upon you. In a world that often equates success and worth with conforming to these expectations, you may find yourself caught between your desires and the roles society prescribes. This internal conflict can create a sense of being torn, a feeling that you're constantly at odds with yourself and the world around you. The absence of a father figure can amplify these tensions, leaving you to maneuver the complex interplay of societal pressures and personal aspirations alone. It's as if you're expected to dance to a tune you've never heard, trying to find your rhythm amid unfamiliar beats.

The ripple effect of an absent father extends beyond personal identity, influencing significant life choices that shape your future. You might find yourself drawn to partners who, consciously or subconsciously, mirror the traits of your absent father, seeking in them the qualities you longed for in him. This can lead to patterns of relationships that echo past dynamics, where the cycle of seeking and not finding repeats itself. The trauma of being abandoned by your father can significantly impact your self-esteem, leading you to believe, consciously or unconsciously, that you are not worthy of love, respect, or stability. As a result, you may gravitate toward men who reflect that inner belief, choosing partners who are emotionally unavailable, unreliable, or even neglectful. The absence of a strong paternal role model can also leave you without a clear standard for a healthy relationship, making it easier to settle for less than you deserve. Over time, this pattern can reinforce the very wounds that started it, creating a cycle of seeking validation from those least capable of providing it.

Career choices, too, can be swayed by the need for stability and validation, driving you toward paths that promise security rather than fulfillment. The absence of paternal guidance can leave you without a clear map, making choices feel like leaps into the unknown without a net to catch you.

Despite these challenges, there are positive pathways to redefining your identity and embracing your individuality in a way that honors your experiences. Self-reflection and journaling can be very helpful and therapeutic in this process, offering you the space to explore your thoughts and feelings without judgment. By engaging in regular self-reflection, you can begin to piece together the fragmented parts of your identity, creating a narrative that is uniquely your own. Journaling allows you to document your journey, capturing insights and revelations illuminating your path. It serves as a mirror, reflecting your inner world and helping you make sense of the nuances within.

Pursuing personal interests and passions is another avenue for embracing your individuality and crafting an identity that feels authentic. Whether it's through art, music, sports, or any other pursuit, these activities allow you to express yourself freely. They encourage you to explore different facets of who you are, unearthing talents and passions that may have lain dormant. Engaging in these pursuits creates a sense of self-discovery and also builds confidence in your abilities and choices. It's about finding joy in the things that make you feel alive, nurturing the aspects of yourself that bring fulfillment and meaning.

As you understand the subtleties and complexities of identity formation, remember that it's a dynamic process that evolves as you grow and learn. The absence of a father figure may have left its mark, but it does not define the entirety of who you are or who you can become. Embrace the opportunity to explore, redefine, and celebrate your identity in all its shades and nuances. In doing so, you can transform the trauma of the past into stepping stones for a future that is as vibrant and multifaceted as the person you are becoming.

Unpacking the Fear of Abandonment

The fear of abandonment is a shadow that often lingers, rooted deeply in the early experiences of those who grew up without a father. It is a fear that can seep into the very essence of your being, affecting how you relate to the world around you. The origins of this fear can often be traced back to early childhood experiences of neglect, where the absence of a consistent paternal figure left a void in the safety and security that a child instinctively seeks. This absence can breed insecurity in attachment to caregivers, leaving you feeling adrift in an unpredictable and unstable world. Without the reassurance of a father's love and presence, the fear that others will leave or abandon you can become an omnipresent concern, casting a long shadow over your interactions and relationships.

As you transition into adulthood, this fear of abandonment can manifest in various and often detrimental ways, particularly in your interpersonal relationships. In romantic relationships, you might cling too tightly to partners, driven by an underlying anxiety that they might leave. This over-dependence can create a dynamic where you sacrifice your own needs and boundaries to keep the relationship intact, fearing that asserting yourself might drive the other person away. Alternatively, you may develop a fear of intimacy or vulnerability, keeping others at arm's length to protect yourself from the potential pain of rejection. This protective mechanism can impede the development of deep, meaningful connections as you struggle to balance the desire for closeness with the fear of loss.

To address and manage this fear of abandonment, it is crucial to engage in strategies that foster healthier relationship dynamics. Practicing open communication with partners is a foundational step, allowing you to express your fears and needs honestly and transparently.

Sharing your vulnerabilities creates an environment where mutual understanding and support can flourish. Developing self-reliance and emotional independence is another important component, as it empowers you to find fulfillment and security within yourself rather than relying solely on external validation. Cultivating hobbies, interests, and a sense of purpose can build a strong sense of self that is resilient to the ebb and flow of relationships.

Therapeutic approaches focusing on attachment styles can provide valuable insights and tools for navigating the complexities of abandonment fears. Exploring these patterns with a therapist can help you understand the root causes of your fears and develop techniques to reframe and manage them. Engaging in therapies such as Cognitive Behavioral Therapy (CBT) or Attachment-Based Therapy can offer structured frameworks for addressing and altering maladaptive beliefs and behaviors, paving the way for healthier relationships and emotional well-being.

Building resilience is integral to overcoming the fear of abandonment and cultivating a secure sense of self. Resilience is not about avoiding challenges but developing the strength and adaptability to face them head-on. Engaging in resilience-building exercises, such as mindfulness practices, can enhance your ability to stay grounded and present, even in uncertainty. Mindfulness encourages you to observe your thoughts and emotions without judgment, allowing you to respond more clearly and calmly. Establishing a strong support network and providing a safety net of understanding and encouragement are equally important. Surrounding yourself with people who recognize and validate your experiences can bolster your confidence and help you manage the dynamics of relationships with greater ease.

As you explore these strategies and build resilience, remember that healing from the fear of abandonment is a gradual process, one that requires patience and compassion for yourself. Each step you take towards understanding and addressing this fear is a testament to your strength and determination to create a life that is not defined by absence but enriched by the connections and experiences you choose to cultivate. The path to overcoming this fear is full of moments of self-discovery and growth, where you learn to trust others and yourself. In embracing this journey, you are laying the foundation for relationships rooted in love, understanding, and mutual respect.

Chapter 2

You stand at a crossroads, shaped by a past where a father's presence was absent. Imagine a young girl with dreams and ambitions yet weighed down by self-doubt. She looks in the mirror, feeling insecure and questioning her worth and where she fits in. This isn't just a story; it's the reality for many daughters who grew up without a father's presence. Feelings of inadequacy and unworthiness can become deeply ingrained, affecting both personal and professional life. The pressure to prove yourself can be exhausting as if your value depends on achievements and outside validation. Over time, self-doubt can become an internal voice that magnifies every perceived flaw. Without a father's love and reassurance, it's easy to fall into the trap of comparing yourself to others who seem to have it all figured out.

In the professional realm, this struggle with self-worth can manifest as hesitation, a reluctance to step into leadership roles, or a reluctance to pursue promotions for fear of being unworthy of success. You might find yourself settling in romantic relationships, accepting less than you deserve because the belief in your own value feels elusive. These choices do not reflect your capabilities or potential but rather the echoes of an ingrained narrative that tells you to stay small to avoid risks that might confirm your deepest fears of inadequacy.

Reclaiming your value begins with recognizing that worth is intrinsic, not contingent upon external validation or comparison. Practicing positive affirmations daily can be a powerful tool in reshaping this narrative, reinforcing the truth that you deserve love, success, and happiness. Create a list of personal strengths and achievements, however small they may seem, and revisit it often. This exercise is a tangible reminder of your capabilities and the unique qualities you bring to the world.

Building self-confidence involves engaging in activities that cultivate competence and self-assurance. Whether it's learning a new skill, pursuing a hobby, or taking on a challenging project at work, each step taken outside your comfort zone is a testament to your strength and resilience. Seek feedback from supportive friends and mentors who recognize your potential and encourage your growth. Their perspectives can offer valuable insights, helping you see the strengths you might overlook in yourself.

Reclaiming Your Value

Take a moment to reflect on your struggles with self-worth. Consider the following questions:

- What are some strengths and qualities that make you unique?

- How have societal pressures influenced your perception of your value?

- In what ways can you begin to prioritize intrinsic value over external validation?

By exploring these questions, you can start dismantling the narratives that have held you back and pave the way for a future defined by confidence and self-acceptance. Your father's absence may have shaped parts of your story, but it does not dictate your worth or your potential. Embrace the opportunity to redefine your value on your terms, unburdened by the shadows of the past.

Building Trust in a World of Doubt

Trust, a cornerstone of human connection, can feel elusive when you've grown up without the reliable presence of a father. This absence often seeds mistrust, an insidious feeling planted early, perhaps when promises were made and broken, or affection was withheld. These early experiences of betrayal or neglect can create a skepticism that extends to authority figures and those in positions of power or care. You may question motives, even without immediate cause for doubt. A silent barrier may arise with each new relationship, a protective mechanism developed over years of learning to anticipate disappointment. While serving as a shield, this skepticism can also isolate you, keeping genuine relationships at bay.

As you navigate adulthood, the mistrust born from an absent father can infiltrate your personal connections, leading to isolation or conflict. It manifests as difficulty in forming deep, meaningful bonds, as you might unconsciously hold back, fearing vulnerability and the potential for hurt. This holding back can feel safer but also lonely. You may find yourself overanalyzing partners' intentions, searching for hidden meanings in their words and actions, convinced that there must be an ulterior motive. This hyper-vigilance, while intended to protect, often drives a wedge between you and those who genuinely care, creating a cycle where mistrust breeds further mistrust. The doubt that once served as armor becomes a barrier, preventing true intimacy and connection.

Rebuilding trust requires intentionality and patience. Begin by practicing transparency in your communication. Share your feelings and fears openly with those you trust, allowing them to understand your perspective and respond with empathy. This openness can lay the groundwork for mutual trust and respect, encouraging an environment where honesty becomes the norm. Establishing healthy boundaries is equally important. Boundaries protect your emotional well-being and ensure interactions are based on respect and understanding. Communicate these boundaries clearly and respect those set by others, recognizing that boundaries are not barriers but frameworks for healthy relationships. Honoring these boundaries creates a space where trust can flourish, gradually replacing the doubt that once dominated.

Cultivating a mindset that embraces trust and openness involves conscious effort. Engage in trust-building exercises with people who have proven themselves reliable, allowing you to explore vulnerability safely. This might include activities that require collaboration or shared decision-making, where the stakes are low but the potential for trust-building is high. Reflecting on past experiences with trusted individuals can also be enlightening. Think about the times when trust was honored, and let those memories be reminders that trust is possible and rewarding. Trust is not about blind faith but informed openness, a willingness to see the good in others while remaining grounded in reality.

Consider incorporating a simple exercise into your routine: a trust journal.

Trust Journal Exercise

In this journal, note instances where trust was either honored or challenged. Reflect on your feelings during these moments and the outcomes that followed. Over time, patterns will emerge, offering insights into your trust dynamics and highlighting areas for growth. This exercise can help you track progress, recognize your triggers, and celebrate small victories in building trust. Each entry becomes a stepping stone towards understanding and reclaiming your ability to trust. By documenting your experiences, you acknowledge the multifaceted aspects of trust while charting a path towards healthier, more fulfilling relationships.

Overcoming Perfectionism: The Quest for Enough

Imagine standing before a canvas, brush in hand, yet paralyzed by the fear of making a single errant stroke. This is the reality of perfectionism, which often takes root in the absence of a father's affirming presence. The presence of a father in a child's life sends the unmistakable message that you have inherent worth. Without a paternal presence to reassure you that imperfection is acceptable and human, you might relentlessly pursue flawless performance, convinced that only perfection will earn you the love and respect you crave. This drive can become all-consuming, where the fear of failure looms large, making every decision fraught with anxiety. You hold yourself to impossibly high standards, fearing that any mistake might confirm your deepest insecurities about not being enough.

The relentless pursuit of perfection comes with a steep price. It can lead to burnout and chronic stress, leaving you exhausted and overwhelmed. The pressure to maintain these unrealistic standards can also strain relationships, as high expectations create tension and disappointment when others inevitably fall short. You might find yourself constantly on edge, unable to relax or enjoy the present moment, as your mind races with thoughts of what needs to be done, fixed, or improved. This constant vigilance takes a toll on your emotional and physical well-being as you strive to keep up with the self-imposed demands of perfectionism.

Embracing imperfection begins with practicing self-compassion, an antidote to the harsh self-criticism that often accompanies perfectionism. Allow yourself the grace to make and learn from mistakes, recognizing that growth usually comes from these imperfect moments. Forgiveness, both for yourself and others, is a powerful tool in this process, freeing you from the burdens of guilt and regret. Set realistic, attainable goals that acknowledge your humanity, allowing room for flexibility and adjustment as needed. Celebrate progress over perfection, recognizing the small victories that contribute to your overall growth and well-being.

Building resilience against perfectionism involves engaging in creative activities without judgment, where the focus is on the process rather than the outcome. Whether it's painting, writing, or playing music, these activities offer a space to explore and express yourself freely, without the constraints of perfectionism. Joining support groups focused on overcoming perfectionism can also provide a sense of community and understanding, where you can share experiences and strategies with others who face similar challenges. These groups offer a safe haven where you can be vulnerable and honest about your struggles, knowing you are not alone in your quest to find balance.

Through these practices, you can begin to loosen the grip of perfectionism, allowing yourself to experience life in all its messy, beautiful gradients. It's about finding peace in the imperfections and understanding that they are what make you uniquely you. Embrace this process of self-discovery and growth, knowing that you are more than your accomplishments and that your worth is not defined by perfection but by the courage to be your authentic self.

Finding Peace with Emotional Isolation

Imagine being in a room full of people but feeling completely alone. This is the reality of emotional isolation, a pervasive feeling that can stem from growing up without a father. You might perceive yourself as different from those around you, carrying the weight of an unspoken trauma that others cannot understand. This sense of being misunderstood can lead to a reluctance to share your feelings as if revealing your inner world might expose you to judgment or rejection. The absence of a father's presence, love, and affirmation can create a barrier to connection, leaving you on the periphery of social interactions, quietly observing but rarely fully participating.

The consequences of prolonged isolation extend beyond emotional discomfort; they can significantly impact your mental and physical health. Feeling isolated can increase the risk of depression and anxiety, as the lack of meaningful connections amplifies feelings of loneliness and despair. Without a support network, crises can feel insurmountable, leaving you to navigate challenges without the comfort and guidance of others. The absence of social support can exacerbate feelings of helplessness as you struggle to find stability in a world that feels indifferent to your struggles. This isolation can become a self-perpetuating cycle, where the fear of reaching out reinforces feeling alone.

Breaking out of this isolation requires intentional efforts to build connections with those around you. Consider participating in community activities that align with your interests; whether it's a book club, sports team, or art class, these gatherings provide opportunities to meet like-minded individuals and form genuine bonds. Volunteering for causes that resonate with your values can also be a powerful way to connect with others while contributing to your community. This shared sense of purpose can create a foundation for lasting relationships as you work alongside others who are passionate about making a difference. Even if it feels daunting at first, initiating one-on-one conversations with trusted individuals can help foster deeper connections. Start with small steps, such as inviting a colleague for coffee or contacting a friend you haven't spoken to in a while. Though seemingly small, these gestures can lead the way for meaningful exchanges and mutual support.

Cultivating inner peace is equally important in overcoming emotional isolation, as it reduces the reliance on external validation and creates a sense of self-sufficiency. Meditation and mindfulness practices offer a path to self-awareness and tranquility, allowing you to observe your thoughts and emotions without judgment. These practices encourage you to be present in the moment, creating a space for reflection and acceptance. Writing can also be a valuable tool for processing emotions and thoughts. By putting pen to paper, you create a dialogue with yourself, exploring your inner world and gaining clarity on your experiences. This reflective practice can reveal patterns and insights guiding you towards healing, as you acknowledge and embrace the emotions shaping your journey.

Reflection Exercise: Finding Peace Within

Take a moment to sit quietly with your thoughts. Consider the following questions as you reflect on your experiences with emotional isolation:

- How has the absence of a father influenced your ability to connect with others?

- What steps can you take to foster meaningful relationships in your life?

- In what ways can you cultivate inner peace and self-acceptance?

By exploring these questions, you begin to understand the layers of isolation and the steps needed to find peace within yourself and with others. The healing journey is about finding strength in your experiences, not attempting to erase the past. Your father's absence may have cast a shadow, but you have the power to step into the light, forging connections that enrich and sustain you.

Breaking the Cycle of Unhealthy Relationships

In the quiet reflections of your past relationships, you might notice recurring patterns that echo the absence of a father's guidance. These patterns often manifest as an attraction to emotionally unavailable partners. Perhaps you've found yourself drawn to those who mirror the emotional distance you experienced in childhood, seeking to fill the void left by your father's absence. This can create a cycle where you're constantly reaching for affection and validation that remains just out of grasp. Such relationships often leave you feeling unfulfilled, as if you're chasing shadows that can never truly be held. The quest for connection becomes a dance of hope and disappointment, where the steps feel all too familiar yet always lead to the same lonely place.

Another common pattern is the tendency to engage in codependent dynamics. Here, you might find yourself sacrificing your own needs and desires to maintain a relationship, believing that your worth is tied to the ability to please and support others. This can lead to an unhealthy balance where your identity becomes enmeshed with your partner's, inhibiting your own self-discovery and independence. The boundaries that should protect your individuality become blurred, leaving you vulnerable to emotional distress. In such dynamics, the focus shifts from mutual respect and growth to a cycle of dependency that stifles both personal and relational development. The fear of abandonment may make you cling tighter, even when the relationship no longer serves your well-being.

Recognizing these patterns is the first step toward change. It requires a willingness to look honestly at your relationships and acknowledge how they echo past wounds. Setting and enforcing personal boundaries becomes imperative. Boundaries are not walls but guidelines that define what you are willing to accept in your relationships. They help you protect your emotional space and ensure interactions are based on mutual respect and understanding. Communicate your boundaries clearly and assertively, and be prepared to respect those set by others. This builds a sense of autonomy and empowers you to make choices that align with your values and needs.

Seeking therapy can also be a transformative step in breaking these cycles. A skilled therapist can help you explore the underlying issues that contribute to unhealthy relationship patterns, offering insights and tools to manage them. Therapy provides a safe space to process your emotions, understand your triggers, and develop strategies for building healthier connections. It can be a path to self-discovery, where you learn to recognize and honor your needs, free from the shadows of the past. Through this work, you can begin to shift the narrative, rewriting the story of your relationships with intention and care.

Building healthy relationship skills involves developing qualities like active listening and empathy. These skills allow you to engage with others in a way that invites genuine connection and understanding.

Practice being fully present in your interactions, listening not just to respond but to truly understand the other person's perspective. This creates a foundation of trust and respect where both parties feel valued and heard. Engage in honest and open communication, sharing your thoughts and feelings with clarity and compassion. This openness invites reciprocity and creates a dynamic where both partners contribute to the growth and vitality of the relationship.

As you learn to break these cycles, remember that change is a gradual process. It requires patience and compassion for yourself as you learn to trust in your ability to create relationships that reflect your true self. Embrace the opportunity to redefine what love and connection mean to you, free from the constraints of past patterns. Each step toward healthier relationships honors your resilience and courage, opening the door to a future filled with authentic and fulfilling connections.

Understanding and addressing these dynamics can transform the way you relate to others, creating a life rich with meaningful relationships that honor your worth and individuality. As you move forward, consider how these insights might influence the next chapter of your life, where the focus shifts from surviving to thriving.

Chapter 3

Growing up in a small town between rolling hills and endless skies, Michelle often looked out of her bedroom window, wondering about the man she had never met. Her mother, a resilient woman who carried the weight of two parents on her shoulders, did her best to fill the void, yet the absence was undeniable.

The reminders of the father-shaped hole in her life were everywhere. Father-daughter dances at school, where she sat on the sidelines watching her friends twirl in their fathers' arms. The handmade Father's Day cards in class that she never had anyone to give to. The lingering pause whenever family tree assignments came up, forcing her to leave half the branches blank. The whispers of children at school, the curious glances from neighbors, and the well-meaning but painful questions from teachers and friends all echoed what was missing.

Michelle's earliest memories included asking her mother about him, questions that lingered in the air like unanswered prayers. "Where is he?" she'd ask, hoping for a story that could paint a picture of the man she could only imagine. Her mother would smile softly, offering reassurances, but the stories were few and far between, leaving Michelle to construct her own narrative from fragments and dreams.

As Michelle moved into her teenage years, her father's absence cast a shadow over her sense of identity and belonging. School became a refuge where she could lose herself in books and activities that offered some semblance of order and predictability. She sought out teachers and mentors, hoping to find the guidance she yearned for in them. Yet, despite their kindness, these figures could never quite fill the void. The search for belonging led her to join various clubs and extracurriculars, hoping that somewhere within the structured chaos of school life, she might find a place where she truly fit in. She joined the drama club, soccer team, and debate team, each offering a sense of community, yet none could fully anchor her drifting sense of self. Her efforts to find a father figure in these environments proved fleeting, as the connections, though meaningful, never quite reached the depth for which she longed. She always felt the absence.

The catalyst for Michelle's transformation came unexpectedly during a school workshop on self-empowerment. A guest speaker, a woman who radiated confidence and warmth, spoke candidly about her own experiences growing up without a father. Her story resonated deeply with Michelle, sparking a realization that she was not alone in her struggles. After the workshop, the woman approached Michelle, sensing a kindred spirit needing guidance. She encouraged Michelle to begin journaling, a practice that helped her process her father's absence and the rippling effects it had on her life. This simple suggestion opened a new world for Michelle, one where she could explore her thoughts and feelings without fear of judgment. The pages of her journal became a sanctuary, a place to unravel the complexities of her emotions and begin piecing together her fractured identity. Michelle found writing to be incredibly therapeutic. She felt safe to write whatever she felt: anger, sadness, resentment, fear, loneliness, pity, and so much more. It really helped her express her emotions without fear of judgment.

As Michelle embraced journaling, she began to uncover a passion for painting, a form of expression that allowed her to communicate what words could not. She explored her emotions with each brushstroke, blending colors and textures to create pieces that spoke to her soul. Painting became another therapeutic outlet, a way to process the feelings that had long been suppressed and festering. The canvas offered a freedom she had never known, a space where she could be unapologetically herself, unburdened by the expectations of others. Through her art, Michelle found a voice that had been silenced for too long, a voice that sang of resilience, strength, and hope.

As she became an adult, Michelle's journey toward self-discovery led her to establish a supportive network of friends who understood and valued her for who she was. These friendships, cultivated through shared interests and mutual respect, provided the emotional support she had longed for. Within this circle, Michelle found acceptance and encouragement, a community where she could grow and flourish. She learned the importance of surrounding herself with people who uplifted and inspired her, believed in her potential, and celebrated her successes. This network became a vital part of her identity, reinforcing the belief that she was worthy of love and belonging.

Finding Your Passion

Consider finding and exploring your own creative outlets or hobbies that resonate with you. Reflect on what activities bring you joy and fulfillment and how they can be a form of self-expression and healing. Write in a journal about your feelings and experiences and how they contribute to your sense of self. Doing these things can help you connect with your inner self, find new ways to process your pain, and turn your ache and longing into a catalyst to propel you forward toward a healthier, happier future.

Michelle's path to empowerment was not easy. She encountered challenges along the way, but her determination to embrace her individuality, build confidence, and feel good about herself proved transformative. She discovered that the absence of a father did not define her but offered an opportunity to write her own story, a story filled with courage, creativity, and connection. Through her experiences, Michelle learned that the power to heal and grow resided within her, a lesson that continues to guide her as she makes her way through life.

Case Study: Healing from Within

In the heart of a bustling city, Beth grew up with her mother, a woman of quiet strength and resilience. Their small apartment was filled with the comforting aroma of home-cooked meals and the steady rhythm of daily life, but no amount of warmth could erase the absence of the father she had never known. He had left before she could form a single memory of him, leaving behind only questions and a void she could never quite fill.

Beth struggled with the contradiction of feeling deeply loved by her mother while aching for a connection that had never existed. The absence of a father became an invisible weight, shaping her in ways she couldn't always articulate. Father's Day at school was a reminder she didn't belong in the same way her classmates did. Hearing friends talk about their dads, about weekend outings, life lessons, and simple moments of affection, made her wonder what she had done to be left behind.

As she grew older, the unanswered questions turned into self-doubt and low self-esteem. She wrestled with feelings of unworthiness, wondering if something about her had made him stay away. The fear of being abandoned seeped into her relationships, making trust difficult. Even when surrounded by love, the shadow of his absence lingered, shaping how she saw herself and the world around her.

Determined to confront the emotional turmoil that had taken root in her life, Beth decided to get professional help and started working with a therapist. Cognitive-behavioral therapy (CBT) became a cornerstone of her healing process. Through CBT, she learned to identify and challenge the negative thought patterns that had been ingrained by years of self-doubt and insecurity. Her therapist guided her through exercises designed to reframe her perceptions, helping her to see herself as whole and worthy despite her father's absence. The sessions offered Beth a structured approach to understanding her emotions and gaining clarity.

In addition to CBT, Beth embraced mindfulness meditation as a means to manage the anxiety that often accompanied her reflections on the past. Mindfulness taught her to stay present, to observe her thoughts without judgment, and to cultivate a sense of peace amidst the chaos. The practice grounded her, allowing her to approach her emotions with gentleness and curiosity rather than fear. Each meditation session was a step towards becoming stronger and more confident, a moment of quiet reflection that helped her center herself in the present, freeing her from the grip of past pain.

The therapeutic process was not without its challenges, but it was also rich with breakthroughs. One significant healing moment came when Beth realized the power of forgiveness, not for her father, but for herself. She understood that holding onto anger and resentment only tethered her to the past, preventing her from embracing the future. Forgiveness became an act of liberation, a way to release his hold on her heart and mind. This realization was profound and impactful, allowing Beth to develop a more compassionate self-view. She began to see herself as resilient and capable, no longer defined by the absence of a father but by the strength she had cultivated in his absence.

The long-term outcomes of Beth's therapy and mindfulness work were incredible. With time, she established healthier relationship patterns, learning to set boundaries and confidently communicate her needs. She became far more confident, and her newfound self-awareness allowed her to engage with others from a place of authenticity, making connections rooted in mutual respect and understanding. The clarity gained through therapy also inspired Beth to give back to her community. She began volunteering with a local organization that supported children facing similar challenges, offering her own experiences as a source of hope and guidance. Through this work, Beth found purpose and fulfillment, channeling her healing into helping others overcome their own family dynamics.

Living with Ghosts: Personal Accounts of Abandonment

In the quiet of a small apartment, Anna sat clutching an old photograph, her fingers tracing its worn edges as if they could bridge the gap between past and present. Her eyes lingered on the image of a man she had never truly known, a father who existed only through fragments of stories passed down by her mother and family friends. His absence had been a shadow in her life, shaping her in ways she could never fully articulate.

She had been just a toddler when he left, too young to form her own memories, yet old enough for his absence to leave an imprint. Over the years, she had pieced together an image of him, not from experience, but from the emotions of those around her. Some spoke of him with fondness, others with resentment, and in their words, Anna found herself caught in a web of contradiction, grappling with a love that was never nurtured and a loss she was never prepared for.

As she grew, this unspoken longing took root in her, manifesting in quiet moments of reflection. She often wrestled with a complex mix of emotions; anger at the void he left behind, sadness for the unanswered questions, and an aching hope that perhaps, one day, she would understand why. The idea of him lingered in her heart like an unfinished story, a presence both comforting and painful.

She turned to writing in her solitude, using poetry to untangle the emotions that had followed her into adulthood. Each line she penned became a small act of healing, a way to give voice to the thoughts she couldn't express aloud. Through her verses, she confronted the wounds of the past, transforming pain into understanding. With each word, she slowly carved out a path toward acceptance, not of the man he was but of the woman she had become despite his absence.

In another part of the world, Leila grew up in a community where family was not just a source of support but a defining aspect of identity. In a place where fathers were seen as protectors and providers, their presence shaped a child's sense of belonging. Without hers, Leila often felt like an outsider, acutely aware of the unspoken assumptions about what a "complete" family should look like. Questions from neighbors and distant relatives, often meant as harmless curiosity, felt like quiet reminders of what was missing.

As she got older, the weight of these cultural expectations only intensified. She saw the way her peers spoke about their fathers with admiration, seeking their guidance and approval. She heard how elders in her community praised young women who embodied traditional roles within their families. Without a father's influence to validate her, she wondered if she was somehow incomplete and if she would always carry a gap that others could sense. The pressure to meet expectations she had no framework for fulfilling made her feel unsteady like she was constantly failing at something she had never been taught.

To escape the frustration and self-doubt, Leila turned to movement. Running became her refuge, a place where no one's opinions could reach her. When she ran, she didn't have to answer questions about her father, explain her family dynamics, or prove her worth through tradition. The rhythm of her steps against the pavement became a source of comfort, a steady beat that drowned out the noise of expectations. With every mile, she felt lighter, as if she were shedding the weight of judgment and reclaiming control over her own story.

Over time, her love for running became more than an escape. It became a way to redefine herself beyond the limitations that had been placed on her. She found strength in her endurance, in the discipline of training, in the moments when her body carried her farther than she thought possible. She didn't need a father's approval to prove her resilience. Through her own determination, she built a sense of self that was no longer defined by what was missing but by the strength she had cultivated on her own.

These personal accounts reveal themes of abandonment and resilience that resonate deeply with daughters who have experienced their father's absence. The stories highlight the myriad of ways individuals cope, each finding unique paths to navigate the emotional landscape left in the wake of a father's departure. For Anna, poetry became a lifeline, a tool for processing complex feelings and finding a voice in silence. For Leila, physical fitness offered a tangible way to reclaim control and foster resilience. These coping mechanisms, though varied, share a common thread of transformation, turning pain into personal growth.

The role of community support emerges as a beacon of hope within these narratives. Anna found solace in the words of other poets, their experiences reflecting her own and offering a sense of connection. In this community, she discovered that her voice was not alone and that others, too, carried the echoes of absent fathers. Similarly, Leila's journey was buoyed by friends who encouraged her pursuits and saw her strength even when she doubted it. These connections, born of shared vulnerability, became pillars of resilience, reinforcing that healing is often a collective endeavor.

The emotional impact of abandonment is undeniable, yet these stories also illuminate the varied strategies employed to cope and thrive. Writing, whether through poetry or journaling, serves as an emotional outlet, providing clarity and release. Physical activities like running or yoga offer physical benefits and mental reprieve, facilitating a connection between body and mind. These strategies highlight the importance of finding personal avenues for expression and healing, acknowledging that the path is deeply individual yet universally significant.

Amid the challenges, lessons of hope and connection shine through, offering a testament to the indomitable human spirit. Many, like Anna, have gone on to build new familial connections in adulthood, creating chosen families that provide the love and support once absent. Leila, inspired by her journey, uses her experiences to advocate for others, sharing her story to uplift and empower those facing similar challenges. These lessons underscore the power of personal strength and the capacity for growth despite adversity. They remind us that while the journey may begin with the shadow of absence, it can lead to a future filled with possibility, connection, and profound resilience.

Voices of Resilience: Stories of Triumph Over Trauma

Resilience often takes root in unexpected places, growing quietly in those who refuse to let their past define them. Monica's story is one of transformation, of turning pain into purpose, loneliness into connection.

From a young age, Monica felt like an outsider, as if something about her was fundamentally wrong. If her own father had chosen to leave, didn't that mean she was unworthy of love? The thought took hold early, shaping the way she saw herself and her place in the world. She watched other children with their fathers, feeling an invisible barrier between them as if they belonged to a club she would never be part of. At family gatherings, when relatives hesitated to mention her father, she felt the weight of his absence press even heavier on her shoulders.

As she grew older, this sense of unworthiness followed her, especially in her interactions with men. She felt uneasy in their presence, always second-guessing herself, unsure how to act. Compliments made her uncomfortable, and any attention, whether kind or indifferent, stirred an anxiety she couldn't explain. Deep down, she believed that if her own father had abandoned her, how could any man see her as valuable? Trusting them felt impossible, as if they, too, would decide she wasn't worth staying for at any moment.

For years, she buried these feelings, ashamed of how deeply they affected her. But the turning point came when she realized she wasn't alone. She met other women who shared the same silent struggles, questions, and lingering pain. Inspired by their stories, Monica decided to create the space she had always needed.

She founded a support group for daughters who had grown up without fathers, a place where they could speak their truth without fear of judgment. Here, they shared their experiences, doubts, and grief. They comforted each other through moments of sadness and celebrated small victories in their healing. What started as a small circle of women soon grew into a community, bound by a shared understanding that none of them had to carry their burden alone.

Through this process, Monica found her own healing. With every conversation, every connection, she began to rewrite the narrative she had believed for so long. She was not broken. She was not unworthy. She had always been enough. And in helping others see their own worth, she finally began to see her own.

Monica wasn't alone in her pursuit of empowerment. Rachel had never met her father. He was absent from her life in every way, leaving behind only a name on a birth certificate and a void she could never fill. His absence wasn't just a fact; it was a wound that had shaped her sense of self from an early age. The trauma of growing up without a father manifested in ways she didn't fully understand at the time. She felt different from her peers, especially when they talked about their dads, about the advice they received, the memories they cherished, the protection they felt. For Rachel, there was nothing but silence where those experiences should have been.

This absence left deep scars. As a child, she internalized the rejection, believing it was her fault, that she wasn't lovable or worthy enough for him to stay. The trauma followed her into adolescence, creating a complete lack of confidence and painfully low self-esteem. She second-guessed herself constantly, afraid to take up space or believe in her own abilities. Every accomplishment felt undeserved, and every failure felt like proof that she wasn't enough. She struggled to trust others, fearing they, too, would eventually leave.

As she grew older, Rachel became determined to understand how her father's absence had shaped her. She turned to education, searching for answers in psychology and human behavior. What started as a personal quest for clarity became a path toward healing and empowerment. Education gave her the tools to name her experiences and recognize that the shame and self-doubt were not hers to carry.

Despite the challenges she faced, Rachel pursued higher education with unwavering determination. She refused to let her trauma define her future. With the support of mentors who saw her potential, she earned her degree and became an advocate for others who had experienced similar pain.

For Rachel, education was more than just knowledge; it was her way of reclaiming her sense of self. Each classroom became a space where she could rebuild her confidence, each lesson a step toward breaking free from the insecurities that had once held her back. Through her pursuit of understanding the psychology of having an absent father, she proved that the absence of a father did not have to mean the absence of a future.

Both Monica and Rachel exemplify strategies that have helped them overcome adversity. Education was a cornerstone for Rachel, while Monica found strength in creating spaces for dialogue and healing. For those in similar situations, seeking mentors and role models can provide invaluable guidance. These figures offer advice and exemplify what is possible when one dares to dream beyond their immediate circumstances. Their insights can illuminate paths previously unseen, offering encouragement and practical wisdom. Engaging with community resources, be it through workshops or educational programs, further reinforces the skills and confidence needed to navigate life's challenges.

Community and support networks played pivotal roles in these stories of resilience. For Monica, the support group she founded became more than just a gathering; it was a passion project and a lifeline. Participating in group therapy sessions provided a sense of belonging and validation, reminding her and others that they were not alone in their experiences. Such environments encourage honesty and vulnerability, allowing participants to confront their feelings head-on. Similarly, Rachel found solace in online forums and support groups, connecting with others who understood her journey. These digital communities offered a platform for sharing struggles and triumphs, building a network of support that transcended geographical boundaries.

Celebrating big and small personal victories forms an integral part of these journeys. Monica witnessed firsthand how members of her support group achieved personal milestones, from mending broken family ties to pursuing long-held dreams. These accomplishments were celebrated collectively, reinforcing that success is sweeter when shared. Rachel's academic achievements marked the beginning of a new chapter, one where her self-doubt was replaced with self-assurance. By continuing to work on self-awareness and growth, both women exemplify the ongoing nature of healing. Their stories remind us that resilience is not a final destination but a continual process of reflection and adaptation.

As these narratives unfold, they paint a vivid picture of triumph over trauma, illustrating that while the absence of a father may cast a long shadow, it need not define one's future. The resilience displayed by Monica, Rachel, and countless others serves as inspiration, highlighting the strength found in community, the power of education, and the importance of self-discovery. These stories are empowering, reminding us that even in the face of adversity, growth and healing are always within reach, waiting to be embraced. In the next chapter, we will explore therapeutic approaches and techniques that further illuminate the path to healing.

Chapter 4

I magine sitting quietly in a room, sunlight filtering through the curtains, a warm cup of tea in your hands. For a brief moment, the outside world fades, and you're fully present. This is mindfulness, a practice that can bring clarity and healing, especially for women struggling with the legacy and fallout of having an absent father.

Mindfulness is simply being present, fully experiencing your thoughts, emotions, and sensations without judgment. It has been practiced for thousands of years through meditation and introspection, but its value today is just as relevant. When dealing with the emotional impact of an absent father, mindfulness can be a powerful tool for emotional regulation, something that often feels out of reach when unresolved feelings take over.

By developing awareness and acceptance, mindfulness helps you acknowledge emotions without being consumed by them. It teaches you to sit with discomfort rather than suppress it, to observe your thoughts without letting them control you. Instead of running from pain or getting lost in self-doubt, mindfulness offers a way to face emotions with curiosity and self-compassion. Over time, it becomes a place of refuge, a way to find clarity and peace amid the uncertainty.

Incorporating mindfulness into your daily routine can be transformative, offering a steady anchor in an unpredictable world. Start with simple breathing exercises, such as focusing on your breath as it flows in and out. This grounding technique can be done anywhere, whether you're at home, work, or out walking. As you breathe deeply, imagine each inhale filling you with calmness and each exhale releasing tension. Mindful walking or eating are also powerful practices. While walking, pay attention to the sensation of your feet touching the ground, or as you eat, notice the flavors and textures with each bite. These practices encourage you to fully engage with the present, creating a sense of peace and presence.

The benefits of mindfulness extend beyond mere relaxation. It has been scientifically proven effective in managing anxiety, reducing stress, and enhancing self-awareness, offering you greater control over your emotional world. By improving emotional resilience, mindfulness allows you to face life's challenges with grace and strength. You'll find that your focus sharpens, enabling you to engage more deeply in daily interactions. Presence becomes a gift you give yourself, a way to enjoy relationships and experiences with authenticity and intention.

Despite its simplicity, mindfulness is not without its challenges. You will probably find your mind wandering during meditation as thoughts intrude like uninvited guests. This is natural, especially when dealing with complex emotions tied to having an absent father. The key is acknowledging these thoughts without judgment and gently returning your focus to the present moment. Creating a dedicated time and space for mindfulness can also enhance your practice. Find a quiet corner, free from distractions, where you can meditate regularly. Consistency is important, as it builds the foundation for mindfulness to flourish in your life.

Mindfulness Breathing Exercise

As you start integrating mindfulness into your daily life, try this simple breathing exercise:

1. Find a Comfortable Position: Sit or lie down in a comfortable position. Close your eyes.

2. Focus on Your Breath: Take a deep breath in through your nose, feeling your chest and abdomen expand. Hold the breath for a moment, and then exhale slowly through your mouth.

3. Count Your Breaths: As you breathe, count each inhale and exhale as one cycle. Focus on the rhythm of your breath and the sensation of air moving in and out of your body.

4. Acknowledge Wandering Thoughts: If your mind begins to wander, gently acknowledge the thought and return your focus to your breath. Remember, there's no right or wrong way to feel during this practice.

5. Continue for Several Minutes: Spend five to ten minutes in this practice, allowing yourself to relax and embrace the present moment.

By incorporating this exercise into your routine, you can begin to experience the calming and restorative effects of mindfulness, clearing the way for healing and emotional growth.

Cognitive-Behavioral Techniques for Emotional Recovery

Growing up abandoned by a father leaves deep emotional scars that don't fade with time. For many girls, this kind of trauma manifests in a relentless lack of confidence, low self-worth, poor self-worth, and a persistent fear of rejection. The absence of a father isn't just a missing presence; it's an unspoken message that can feel like proof of being unlovable or unworthy. These wounds shape how a daughter views herself and the world, making trust difficult and self-confidence nearly impossible. Women carrying this trauma often cannot stand up for themselves and accept far less than they should in relationships, especially romantic relationships.

The trauma of father abandonment can lead to deeply ingrained negative thought patterns, reinforcing beliefs like, *I'm not good enough, People always leave,* or *I will never succeed.* These thoughts feel real because they have existed for so long, shaping identity and behavior. This is where Cognitive-Behavioral Therapy (CBT) becomes essential. CBT offers a way to break the cycle of self-destructive thinking by identifying, challenging, and replacing harmful beliefs with healthier, more realistic ones.

One of the core principles of CBT is recognizing cognitive distortions and irrational thought patterns that convince you of falsehoods, such as believing you're inherently unworthy of love or success. These distortions become a lens through which you see the world, reinforcing negative emotions and behaviors. CBT helps dismantle these beliefs by examining the evidence behind them. Are these thoughts based on facts, or do fear and past trauma drive them?

Through structured exercises, CBT provides tools to rebuild self-worth. Journaling, thought-challenging techniques, and guided role-playing help reframe damaging beliefs. For example, suppose the thought *I will never be good enough* arises. In that case, CBT encourages identifying times when you *were* enough, when you succeeded, when someone valued you, or when you showed resilience. Over time,

these exercises rewire the brain, making self-compassion and confidence more accessible.

Father abandonment trauma doesn't have to dictate the rest of your
life. CBT offers a way to take control, rewrite your inner narrative,
and break free from the patterns of self-doubt and emotional pain that
have kept you stuck.

Self-monitoring plays an important role in CBT. It involves keeping
track of your thoughts and behaviors and creating a feedback loop
that aids in emotional recovery. Journaling is a powerful tool here.
By writing down your thoughts, you gain insights into patterns and
triggers. It creates a space for honest reflection, allowing you to see the
progress you might not notice day-to-day. Thought records, another
CBT tool, help you track how your thoughts lead to certain emotions
and actions. By regularly reviewing these records, you can identify
areas for change and celebrate small victories.

Over time, consistent practice of CBT techniques can lead to
long-term emotional well-being. Start by setting realistic goals for personal development. Perhaps it's becoming more assertive or reducing
anxiety in social situations. Breaking these goals into smaller, manageable steps makes them less daunting and more achievable. As you
work towards these goals, celebrate incremental achievements. Each
step forward, no matter how small, is a victory. It's a testament to your
strength and resilience, a reminder that change is possible.

CBT doesn't just offer a temporary fix. It gives you a toolkit for life,
enabling you to face challenges confidently and clearly. You learn to
manage your emotions, not by avoiding them, but by understanding
and transforming them. Through this process, you gain a deeper insight into yourself, recognizing your potential and worth. The path
of CBT is not always easy, but it is rewarding. By embracing its techniques, you open the door to a future where you're not defined by

growing up without a father but by the presence of your strength and capacity for growth.

The Power of Narrative Therapy

Imagine standing at the edge of a dense forest, where each tree represents a story from your life. Narrative therapy invites you to walk through this forest, not as a passive observer but as the storyteller. It's a therapeutic approach that recognizes you as the author of your own life story, with the power to reframe and rewrite the narratives that have defined you. For women who grew up without a father, the story often begins with a void, a sense of absence that colors each chapter. Narrative therapy helps you explore how these dominant narratives, often laden with themes of abandonment or unworthiness, have shaped your self-perception and life choices.

At the heart of narrative therapy is the concept of re-authoring your story. This involves identifying the dominant narratives limiting your growth and crafting alternative ones highlighting your resilience and strength. You begin by examining the stories you've told yourself about your father's absence. Are these stories of rejection and abandonment, or do they acknowledge the courage and resourcefulness you've demonstrated in their wake? By recognizing these narratives, you can start making new stories that celebrate your perseverance and adaptability. These new narratives don't erase the past but integrate it into a broader, more empowering view of who you are and who you can become.

Narrative therapy employs various techniques to facilitate this process of re-authoring. One such technique is externalizing problems, which involves viewing issues as separate from your identity. For instance, instead of internalizing the absence of a father as a personal failing, you might see it as a challenge you've navigated with resilience. This shift in perspective can be liberating, allowing you to address problems without feeling defined by them. Another technique involves using metaphors and symbols in storytelling. These creative elements can unlock deeper insights, helping you articulate complex emotions and experiences in a way that feels meaningful and accessible.

The benefits of narrative therapy are profound, offering a pathway to enhanced self-awareness and emotional healing. Through this therapeutic lens, you develop a stronger sense of identity and purpose grounded in a narrative that honors your experiences. You learn to see yourself not as a victim of circumstances but as an active participant in shaping your life. This empowerment creates a narrative of hope, where possibilities replace limitations, and where your story becomes one of growth and potential. As you engage with narrative therapy, you can explore the richness of your life, recognizing that you hold the pen and can write new chapters filled with promise and possibility.

Exploring Creative Expression as Therapy

Imagine a canvas before you, blank and full of potential, much like the emotions stirred by the absence of a father. Creative expression serves as a therapeutic outlet, a space where emotions can be explored and released without the constraints of language. For many, engaging in creative activities offers cathartic relief, helping to process emotions that might otherwise remain tangled and unspoken. In its many forms, art becomes a conduit for self-expression, allowing you to communicate the complexities of your inner world. Whether through painting, music, or writing, creative expression provides a safe haven to explore feelings of anger, sadness, or longing, transforming them into something tangible and meaningful.

Various creative therapies cater to individual needs, each offering unique pathways to emotional release and healing. Art therapy, for instance, focuses on visual expression, enabling you to capture and reflect your emotions through colors, shapes, and textures. It provides a non-verbal medium that can be particularly powerful when words fall short. Music and dance therapy, on the other hand, harness the power of rhythm and movement to facilitate emotional release. These therapies tap into the body's natural rhythms, allowing you to express feelings through sound and motion, often leading to profound emotional shifts. Writing therapy invites reflective exploration, where writing helps unravel the narratives that shape your experience. Through journaling or storytelling, you can gain insights into your thoughts and emotions, crafting narratives that honor your journey and highlight your resilience.

Incorporating creativity into daily life doesn't have to be daunting. Setting aside time for creative journaling can be a simple yet effective way to engage with your emotions regularly. This practice allows you to explore thoughts and feelings at your own pace, offering a space for reflection and growth. Consider participating in community art projects or workshops where you can connect with others while exploring your creative side. These shared experiences build a sense of belonging and support, reminding you that you're not alone in your struggles. The key is finding activities that resonate with you, whether sketching, writing poetry, or playing an instrument. The goal is not perfection but expression, providing an outlet for emotions that might otherwise remain suppressed.

Overcoming barriers to creativity involves confronting the perfectionism that can stifle expression. It's easy to fall into the trap of believing that creative endeavors must meet certain standards, but this mindset can hinder the healing you seek. Letting go of perfectionism means allowing yourself the freedom to create without judgment, embracing the process rather than the outcome. Explore new creative mediums without fear of failure, approaching each with curiosity and openness. Remember, creativity is about self-expression, not comparison. By focusing on the joy of creating rather than the final product, you open the door to healing and growth. Embrace the imperfections, the smudges, and the off-key notes, for they are part of your unique expression. Through creative therapy, you can find solace and strength, turning the absence of a father into a wellspring of inspiration and empowerment.

Building a Supportive Therapeutic Relationship

Imagine walking into a room where you feel completely at ease, where the air is filled with understanding rather than judgment. This is the essence of a supportive therapeutic relationship, an essential component in healing from the wounds left by an absent father. Establishing trust and safety in therapy is paramount, as it lays the foundation for genuine exploration and healing. Trust allows you to open up and share your deepest fears and hopes, knowing you are met with empathy and active listening. These elements transform the therapeutic setting into a sanctuary where vulnerability is met with compassion and your voice is heard and valued. The bond between you and your therapist becomes a partnership, one that supports and nurtures your journey toward self-discovery and healing.

Choosing the right therapist is the most important step in this process, particularly when processing the complexities of father-related trauma. It's important to find someone who possesses the necessary expertise and understands the nuances of your experiences. Look for key qualities such as empathy, patience, and an open-minded approach. During initial consultations, don't hesitate to ask questions that help you gauge their understanding of and sensitivity to issues related to absent fathers. Specifically, ask about their experience with similar cases, their therapeutic approach, and how they envision supporting your healing process. Remember, this is your effort to heal your trauma and move forward to a healthier life, and finding the right guide is essential to its success. The right therapist will provide guidance and empower you to explore and understand your emotions more deeply.

Once you've found a therapist you feel comfortable with, building a collaborative and open relationship is imperative for effective healing. This means actively engaging in setting goals and expectations with your therapist, ensuring that both of you are aligned in your approach and objectives. Discuss what you hope to achieve through therapy and consider how you will measure progress together. Honest communication about therapy progress is equally important. If certain strategies aren't working for you or if you feel stuck, express these concerns. A good therapist will welcome this dialogue, adjusting their approach to better meet your needs. This collaboration transforms the therapeutic process into a dynamic and evolving journey, one where your input and insights are integral to the path forward.

Maintaining progress outside of therapy sessions is another key component of effective healing. The skills and insights you gain in therapy are most beneficial when they are applied in real-life situations. Practice and apply these skills regularly, whether it's using grounding techniques during moments of anxiety or employing communication strategies in relationships. This application reinforces what you've learned, integrating it into your daily life. Regularly revisiting therapeutic goals and achievements can also be motivating, reminding you of how far you've come and the growth you've experienced. Celebrate these milestones, no matter how small, as they are markers of your resilience and determination. This continuous practice and reflection ensure that the therapeutic benefits extend beyond the confines of sessions, enriching your life in meaningful and lasting ways.

As you cultivate a supportive therapeutic relationship, you're investing in your healing and your future. This partnership offers the tools and insights needed to handle the complexities of emotions tied to the trauma and subsequent fallout of having an absent father. It's a commitment to yourself and your well-being, a promise to nurture and honor your journey toward wholeness. As you carry these lessons forward, remember that the strength to heal lies within you, supported by those who walk alongside you in this transformative process. You are learning to respond to your circumstances instead of reacting to them; this is very powerful.

Chapter 5

Growing up without a father leaves an imprint that extends far beyond childhood. For many women, his absence creates a deep need to prove their worth, as if achieving enough, being enough, or excelling enough could somehow compensate for the void he left behind. Perfectionism becomes more than just a personality trait; it becomes a survival mechanism. It is a way to control what once felt uncontrollable, to seek validation where it was never freely given, and to construct an identity built on achievement rather than inherent worth.

The link between fatherlessness and perfectionism is strong. When a father is absent, whether physically or emotionally, his daughter is left with questions that often remain unanswered: *Why wasn't I enough for him to stay? Was it something about me?* These silent fears take root, growing into a belief that love and acceptance must be earned. Perfectionism becomes the answer to an unspoken question: *If I am flawless, will I finally be worthy?*

This relentless pursuit of perfection can manifest in all areas of life. In work, it may present as an obsession with overachievement, setting impossibly high standards, overworking, and feeling that any mistake is proof of inadequacy. A woman may refuse to delegate tasks, fearing that someone else's failure will reflect poorly on her. At home, perfectionism may take the form of hyper-independence, an unwillingness to ask for help, and a constant drive to have everything under control. Relationships often suffer, as perfectionism breeds an underlying fear of vulnerability. Letting someone see flaws or weaknesses feels like a risk too great to take; after all, wasn't imperfection what led to abandonment in the first place?

Cultural and familial expectations further reinforce these patterns. Society often places immense pressure on women to excel, be strong, and be both accomplished and nurturing. For a woman who grew up without a father, this pressure compounds an already internalized belief: that she must be extraordinary to be worthy of love. The bar is set impossibly high, yet she continues reaching for it, afraid that slowing down or making a mistake will confirm the very fears she has spent a lifetime trying to outrun.

But perfectionism is a double-edged sword. While it may provide a temporary sense of control, it also creates a cage, one built of self-criticism, unrealistic standards, and chronic anxiety. The constant pressure to excel can lead to exhaustion, burnout, and an inability to ever feel satisfied with success. The voice of perfectionism is never content; no matter how much is achieved, the bar simply moves higher.

Cognitive-Behavioral Therapy (CBT) offers a path toward breaking free from this cycle. It helps uncover the thought patterns that fuel perfectionism, such as the belief that worth is tied to accomplishments or that any mistake equals failure. CBT encourages questioning these beliefs: *Is it true that I am only valuable if I am perfect? What evidence do I have to support that?* Over time, this process rewires the brain to recognize that self-worth is not dependent on external validation.

One of the most powerful tools in CBT is tracking perfectionistic thoughts. Writing them down, whether in a journal or through structured exercises—can reveal patterns and triggers reinforcing unhealthy behaviors. For instance, if a woman thinks, *If I don't do this perfectly, I will be judged or rejected,* she can begin to challenge that assumption. Where did this belief originate? What would happen if she allowed herself to be imperfect? These distorted thoughts lose their grip through consistent practice, making space for self-compassion and acceptance.

Physical symptoms can also be key indicators of perfectionism's toll; chronic tension, headaches, fatigue, and even digestive issues often arise from the constant stress of trying to meet impossible standards. Learning to recognize these signs can serve as a wake-up call, a reminder to step back and reassess.

Healing from the perfectionism born out of father abandonment is not about lowering standards. It is about releasing the belief that perfection is the price of love and belonging. It is about recognizing that worth is inherent, not conditional. It is about learning to embrace imperfections, not as failures but as proof of being human. Through CBT and intentional self-reflection, it is possible to break free from the grip of perfectionism and reclaim a sense of self-worth that no longer depends on being flawless.

Uncovering Perfectionistic Patterns

Take a moment to reflect on your experiences with perfectionism. Consider the following journaling prompts:

- What situations trigger your perfectionistic tendencies?

- How do you feel when you believe you haven't met your own standards?

- In what ways does perfectionism impact your relationships and work?

- What steps can you take to challenge and reframe perfectionistic thoughts?

This exercise can help you gain clarity and identify actionable steps towards healing and growth. By understanding the patterns of perfectionism, you can begin to embrace a more balanced and fulfilling life that honors your worth beyond achievements. As you go through this process, remember that healing is about finding strength in your experiences and choosing a new path forward, not about erasing the past.

Releasing the Need to Overachieve

Have you ever found yourself chasing one goal after another, convinced that the next achievement will finally prove your worth? This relentless pursuit of success often stems from a desire to compensate for feelings of inadequacy, particularly when a father's presence was absent during crucial developmental years. When self-worth becomes intertwined with accomplishments, you may find yourself trapped in a cycle where each success only temporarily fills the void, leading to a relentless work ethic fueled by the fear of failure. This drive to overachieve can become an identity, a way to shield yourself from the vulnerability of feeling less than. Yet, relying on external achievements to define your value can lead to an exhausting and never-ending chase.

The costs of overachievement extend beyond personal exhaustion; they seep into relationships and well-being. Workaholism, often a byproduct of overachievement, can lead to neglected relationships as work becomes the priority over family, friends, and personal connections. The demands of maintaining a high performance level can make it difficult to engage meaningfully with those around you, leaving loved ones feeling sidelined. As the commitments pile up, health and well-being may take a backseat. Late nights, skipped meals, and constant stress can lead to physical ailments, while mental fatigue becomes a constant companion. What once might have been a source of joy and passion becomes a source of pressure and stress, leaving little room for leisure activities or hobbies that were once cherished. The simple pleasures of life, the activities done purely for enjoyment, can lose their luster when overshadowed by the drive to achieve. The cost is not just in the relationships that fray or the health that suffers but in the missed moments of joy and connection that life offers.

To release the grip of overachievement, you can start by setting realistic and flexible goals. These goals should reflect what you want to accomplish and what brings you joy and fulfillment. Flexibility is key, allowing room for adjustments as life unfolds. This approach acknowledges that while goals are important, they should not overshadow the experience of living. Prioritizing tasks and delegating responsibilities is another step toward balance. By focusing on what truly matters and letting go of the need to control every detail, you create space for other aspects of life. Delegation can be daunting, especially when self-worth is tied to doing everything yourself, but it is a foundational step in building trust and collaboration with others. It allows you to step back and see the bigger picture, recognizing that success is not just about personal achievements but also about the collective efforts of those you surround yourself with.

Embracing non-achievement is an art that involves finding value in activities not tied to goals or success. Engaging in leisure activities purely for enjoyment, without the pressure of performance, can be liberating. Whether it's reading a book, taking a walk, or exploring a new hobby, these moments remind you of life's simple joys. Practicing gratitude for everyday experiences helps shift the focus from what you lack to what you have. By appreciating the small moments, like a sunrise, a shared meal, or a conversation with a friend, you create a sense of fulfillment that is not reliant on external validation. Gratitude leads to contentment, allowing you to recognize and cherish the richness of life beyond accomplishments.

Consider keeping a "joy journal," where you note moments of happiness and gratitude each day. Reflect on these entries to remind yourself of the abundance in your life, independent of professional or personal achievements. This practice can serve as a powerful reminder that your worth is not measured by what you do but by who you are. It encourages you to celebrate the person you are becoming, not just the milestones you reach. Embracing this perspective can transform the way you approach life, shifting from a focus on doing to a focus on being. In this space, you find freedom from the confines of overachievement, allowing you to live authentically and fully.

Embracing Vulnerability: A Path to Authenticity

For women who grew up without a father, vulnerability often feels like a risk too great to take. When the very person who was supposed to provide protection, love, and security was absent, the lesson learned early was that people leave, and trusting others can lead to pain. As a result, many daughters of absent fathers build walls, equating emotional self-sufficiency with strength and viewing vulnerability as a weakness. Yet, true strength lies in allowing oneself to be seen, to be known, and to connect with others without the constant fear of rejection. Vulnerability is not a flaw, it is the key to breaking free from the patterns of emotional isolation that fatherlessness can create.

For women who have spent years striving for independence as a means of survival, the idea of vulnerability can feel foreign, even dangerous. Growing up without a father can create a deep-seated fear of abandonment, leading to a belief that if you show your true self, your fears, insecurities, and struggles, you will be left behind again. This fear drives many to overcompensate, adopting a persona of perfection, strength, or emotional detachment to guard against further rejection. The result is a life where relationships remain surface-level, intimacy is avoided, and loneliness persists despite outward success.

Society reinforces this defense mechanism, particularly for women raised without fathers, by valuing resilience and self-reliance over emotional openness. Many daughters of absent fathers are taught, explicitly or implicitly, that they must be strong enough to handle everything alone, that needing others is a sign of weakness, and that emotions must be kept in check. But this kind of emotional self-protection, while understandable, ultimately prevents real connection. It keeps love, support, and understanding at a distance, even when those things are deeply craved.

The way forward toward embracing vulnerability starts with recognizing that it is not the enemy, it is a bridge to healing. Acknowledging the pain of growing up fatherless, rather than suppressing it, is an act of courage. This does not mean reliving the past but instead allowing yourself to feel, process, and accept that the absence of a father shaped you, but it does not have to define you. Cognitive-Behavioral Therapy (CBT) and other forms of self-reflection can help challenge the belief that vulnerability leads to abandonment or rejection. Instead of assuming that openness will push people away, it becomes possible to see that authenticity fosters deeper, more meaningful connections.

Creating safe spaces to practice vulnerability is crucial. Start small, sharing your thoughts and feelings with people who have proven trustworthy and understanding. Whether it's a close friend, a therapist, or a support group, these are the people who will hold your emotions with care, showing you that opening up does not always lead to pain. Engaging in activities that push you outside your comfort zone, whether creative expression, personal writing, or conversations about your past, can also help build confidence in expressing your true self. Each step, no matter how small, is a step toward breaking the cycle of emotional isolation.

The benefits of embracing vulnerability are profound. Allowing yourself to be seen for who you truly are fosters self-acceptance, breaking the exhausting cycle of seeking external validation. No longer needing to prove your worth through perfection or emotional detachment, you can begin to cultivate a sense of inner peace. Relationships deepen, as authenticity invites authenticity. When you allow yourself to be open, others feel safe doing the same, creating bonds built on mutual trust rather than guarded facades.

Healing from the emotional wounds of fatherlessness does not mean erasing the past, it means allowing yourself to live beyond it. Vulnerability is not weakness; it is a declaration that you are worthy of love, connection, and acceptance exactly as you are. It is the willingness to let go of the armor that once protected you but now only keeps you isolated. Choosing vulnerability is choosing freedom—the freedom to live fully, love deeply, and no longer let a father's absence dictate the presence of fear.

Self-Compassion: Healing Through Kindness

Imagine offering yourself the same kindness you would extend to a close friend. This is the heart of self-compassion. It's about treating yourself with warmth and understanding, particularly during moments of failure or inadequacy. When you've grown up without the presence of a father, it can be easy to internalize feelings of unworthiness, to believe that you must earn love and acceptance. Self-compassion challenges this narrative by recognizing that imperfection is a shared human experience, not a personal failing. It invites you to acknowledge your struggles without harsh judgment, paving the way for healing and acceptance.

Practicing self-compassion can be challenging, especially when internalized voices of criticism and judgment are loud. These voices may tell you that you're not enough, that you must strive harder to be worthy. They are often echoes of cultural messages that equate self-compassion with weakness, as if being kind to oneself is indulgent or undeserved. Such misconceptions can create barriers, convincing you that self-compassion is not a valid or effective approach to healing. Yet, these messages overlook the strength found in gentleness, the resilience that comes from embracing one's humanity with kindness. Recognizing these barriers is the first step towards breaking them down, allowing self-compassion to flourish.

There are tangible ways to cultivate self-compassion in your daily life, transforming it from an abstract concept into a lived experience. One powerful exercise is writing compassionate letters to yourself. You might think this is a silly exercise, but try it; it helps and is very empowering. In these letters, speak to yourself with the same empathy and encouragement you would offer a dear friend. Acknowledge your struggles and celebrate your strengths, reinforcing the message that you are deserving of love and kindness. This practice can be particularly healing when facing difficult emotions or reflecting on past experiences. Another effective technique is loving-kindness meditation, where you silently repeat phrases of goodwill and compassion towards yourself and others. This meditation creates a sense of interconnectedness, reminding you that you are part of a larger human community, all navigating the complexities of life together.

The effects of self-compassion extend beyond immediate emotional relief; they can transform your mental and emotional well-being over time. By embracing self-compassion, you begin to rewrite the narrative of self-worth, shifting from external validation to intrinsic value. This shift brings a sense of inner peace, where you no longer feel the need to prove yourself to others or meet unattainable standards. Instead, you cultivate a deep sense of self-acceptance, recognizing that you are enough, just as you are. This acceptance does not mean complacency; it empowers you to grow and learn from a place of love and understanding. As self-compassion becomes a guiding force in your life, it opens the door to deeper connections with others as you approach relationships with empathy and authenticity.

Incorporating self-compassion into your life is a gentle exploration, where you learn and handle the nuances of your emotions with grace and kindness. Each moment of self-compassion is a step towards healing, a testament to your resilience and capacity for growth. As you embrace this practice, you will find that it enriches your life in profound ways, offering a foundation of love and acceptance that supports you through life's challenges. This chapter's exploration of self-compassion leads naturally into the next, where we will dive into the importance of building strong, supportive relationships that nurture and sustain you on your path.

Chapter 6

I magine walking through a crowded room, surrounded by laughter and lively conversation, yet feeling an invisible wall between yourself and everyone else. This sense of isolation can stem from patterns developed in childhood, particularly when a father is absent. For daughters growing up without their fathers, this absence can leave an emotional void that significantly impacts their relationships. Without a father's presence and guidance, these girls often learn to cope with the world and their emotions in ways that don't always serve their well-being. They may grow up seeking connection in ways that mirror the unfilled space in their lives, leading to unhealthy relational patterns like codependency and emotional unavailability.

The longing for a father's love and validation often transforms into a deep need to fill that void in relationships. In some cases, this manifests as codependency, where boundaries between self and others blur. You may find yourself prioritizing someone else's needs above your own, feeling that your worth is only validated by what you do for others. In this dynamic, your identity may become intertwined with the needs of your partner, leaving you emotionally drained and dependent on their approval. For many daughters without fathers, this can be an unconscious attempt to recreate the stability and love they lacked as children, but it often leads to imbalanced, unhealthy relationships where their own needs are neglected.

On the other hand, emotional unavailability can be a protective mechanism developed to shield oneself from the pain of abandonment. If your father wasn't around, the fear of opening up to others can become paralyzing. Keeping people at arm's length becomes a way to guard against the possibility of being hurt or rejected once again. You may emotionally shut down or distance yourself from others, fearing that letting anyone in could result in the same kind of disappointment or abandonment you experienced with your father.

Recognizing the red flags in relationships is the first step to breaking free from these deeply ingrained patterns. For daughters who grew up without their fathers, a key sign of unhealthy relationship dynamics is over-dependence. You may find yourself relying too heavily on a partner for emotional support, feeling lost or incomplete without their constant presence or approval. This emotional reliance can create a sense of imbalance, where your entire sense of self becomes tied to another person's validation, leaving you feeling lost or powerless without them. Another warning sign is the cycle of repeated conflicts. The same arguments and unresolved issues often resurface, leaving you feeling stuck in an endless loop of tension and dissatisfaction. These cycles can sap your energy, making it difficult to break free and find peace in your relationships.

The toll these unhealthy dynamics can take is far-reaching. Emotionally, you may experience burnout, feeling drained from constantly trying to meet others' needs while ignoring your own. This exhaustion can lead to feelings of anxiety, depression, or irritability, as you struggle to maintain a balance in relationships that never truly gives back. Over time, your sense of self can erode as you lose sight of who you are outside the context of the relationship. The emotional wounds from your father's absence may manifest in confusion, feelings of emptiness, or an inability to connect with your true self. These patterns can prevent you from growing and healing, making it difficult to move forward and create the fulfilling relationships you deserve.

To break free from these cycles, it's important to engage in deep self-reflection. Journaling can be a powerful tool, allowing you to explore your emotions and past experiences without judgment. Take time to reflect on past relationships and identify recurring patterns. What unmet needs have driven your choices in these relationships? How have these dynamics aligned with or contradicted your values? This type of reflection can help you identify areas for growth and give you the clarity you need to move toward healthier ways of connecting with others. Additionally, seeking feedback from trusted friends can provide valuable perspective. Those who know you well can help identify patterns or blind spots you might not be able to see on your own. Open, honest conversations with loved ones can offer insights and guidance, empowering you to break free from old habits and step into a healthier way of relating to yourself and others.

Relationship Patterns Checklist

Take a moment to assess your relationship dynamics with this checklist. Reflect on each statement and consider how it applies to your relationships. Consider how this may be influenced by your father not being in your life:

1. I often feel responsible for my partner's happiness.

2. I struggle to say "no" to my partner, even when it compromises my own needs.

3. I find myself repeating the same arguments with my partner

without resolution.

4. I feel anxious or incomplete when my partner is not around.

5. My sense of self-worth is heavily influenced by my partner's approval.

If you identify with several of these statements, it may be helpful to explore these patterns further with a therapist or counselor. This checklist is a starting point for reflection, offering a framework to understand and address the dynamics at play in your relationships.

Emotional Isolation: Bridging the Gap

Growing up without a father can often lead to emotional isolation, a state where you feel disconnected from those around you, even in a crowded room. This isolation stems from a fear of vulnerability, where opening up seems risky, as if baring your soul might lead to judgment or rejection. Without a paternal figure to model healthy emotional expression, you may have developed an armor, a shield to protect against the hurt of potential abandonment. This fear is compounded by the misunderstanding you might encounter from peers who cannot fathom the depth of your internal struggle. They see the surface, the smiles, and the laughter, but rarely recognize the loneliness that lingers beneath. This misunderstanding can create a chasm between you and others, reinforcing the belief that you are somehow different, somehow apart.

The emotional toll of isolation is profound. It can lead to increased feelings of loneliness, where even amidst friends, you feel like an outsider looking in. This loneliness can become a breeding ground for self-doubt as you question why connection seems so elusive. The difficulty in forming deep connections often stems from a reluctance to let others in, a protective measure that keeps you safe yet isolated. This reluctance can manifest as surface-level relationships, where interactions remain shallow, lacking the depth and understanding that foster true intimacy. Over time, the weight of this isolation can erode your emotional well-being, leading to a sense of emptiness and despair. The absence of meaningful connections can leave you adrift, yearning for a sense of belonging that feels just out of reach.

To bridge this emotional gap, consider developing active listening skills, which can transform your interactions with others. Active listening is more than hearing words; it's about engaging with the speaker, showing empathy and understanding. By practicing this, you not only deepen your connections but also invite others to reciprocate, creating a space where vulnerability is welcomed and cherished. Joining clubs or community groups can also provide a fertile ground for building relationships. These environments offer shared interests and goals, a natural foundation for connection. Whether it's a book club, a sports team, or a volunteer group, these settings encourage interactions that go beyond the superficial, fostering bonds that are rooted in common experiences and mutual support.

Building a supportive network of friends and family is crucial in overcoming emotional isolation. Finding a support group can offer a sense of community and understanding, where your experiences are validated and shared by others. These groups provide a platform for honest conversations where you can explore your feelings without fear of judgment. Reaching out to family members, even if relationships have been strained, can also be a step toward healing. Family ties, though complex, often hold the potential for reconciliation and support. By taking the initiative to reconnect, you open the door to rebuilding relationships that may have been affected by your father's absence. These connections, whether familial or chosen, form the backbone of your support network, offering the love and acceptance that can help dissolve the barriers of isolation.

Identity Confusion: Discovering Your True Self

Growing up as a daughter without a father can often lead to a deep sense of emotional isolation, where you feel disconnected from those around you, even in the midst of a crowd. The absence of a paternal figure leaves a void, and this isolation is compounded by a fear of vulnerability that stems from the emotional gap left by your father. Opening up feels risky, as though exposing your true self might invite judgment or rejection. Without a father to model healthy emotional expression, you may have unknowingly built a wall around your heart, a protective shield designed to guard against the pain of abandonment. This fear is often misunderstood by those around you, who might not grasp the depth of your internal struggle. They see your outward smile and hear your laughter, but they don't see the loneliness that quietly lingers beneath the surface. This misunderstanding can create a growing distance between you and others, reinforcing a belief that you are somehow different, somehow separate.

The emotional toll of growing up without a father and experiencing this isolation can be profound. Even when surrounded by friends, you may feel like an outsider looking in, unable to connect in a way that truly satisfies your need for closeness. This persistent loneliness can lead to self-doubt, as you question why genuine connection feels so elusive. The difficulty in forming deep, meaningful relationships often stems from an unwillingness to let others get too close, a defense mechanism developed to shield yourself from the possibility of further abandonment. This reluctance can result in shallow interactions, where the bonds you form are more superficial than authentic, lacking the intimacy and understanding that nourish real connection. Over time, this emotional isolation can begin to erode your sense of self-worth, leaving you feeling adrift and uncertain about your place in the world. The absence of a father's love and guidance can make it feel as though you are constantly searching for a sense of belonging that seems just beyond your reach.

To bridge this emotional divide and overcome isolation, developing active listening skills can be transformative. Active listening goes beyond simply hearing words, it involves fully engaging with others, showing empathy, and offering understanding. By practicing active listening, you invite others to open up, creating a space where vulnerability is welcomed and mutual trust can flourish. This can deepen your relationships and help to heal the emotional scars left by your father's absence. Engaging in community activities, such as joining a book club, sports team, or volunteer group, can also provide a fertile ground for forming meaningful connections. These shared experiences offer a natural foundation for bonding, where interactions move beyond surface-level conversations and evolve into genuine, supportive relationships.

Building a supportive network of friends and family is a must in order to overcome emotional isolation. Seeking out a support group can provide a safe space where your experiences are understood and validated by others who have walked a similar path. These groups allow for honest conversations and self-expression, offering a sense of belonging that may have been missing for years. Reaching out to family members, even if past relationships have been strained due to your father's absence, can also be a healing step. While complex, family ties often hold the potential for reconciliation, offering a chance to rebuild connections that may have been affected by the emotional void left by your father. These relationships, whether with family or chosen friends, form the foundation of a strong support network, offering the love, acceptance, and emotional nourishment needed to break free from the isolation that often follows growing up without a father.

Longing for Validation: Finding Self-Acceptance

Growing up without a father can create a profound longing for validation, a yearning for the approval and acknowledgment that feels elusive. This desire often stems from a place of insecurity, where the neglect or absence of a father leaves a void that you're constantly trying to fill. Without that paternal figure to affirm your worth, you might turn outward, seeking validation from others to affirm what feels missing within. This external search becomes a way to compensate for feelings of inadequacy, a hope that someone else's approval can quiet the doubts and insecurities that linger. It's a common narrative among daughters of absent fathers, where the need for external recognition becomes intertwined with your sense of self.

Relying on external validation for self-worth, however, is like building a house on shifting sands. The confidence it brings is often short-lived, a fleeting boost that dissipates as quickly as it arrives. When your worth hinges on others' opinions, you find yourself on a perpetual rollercoaster, rising and falling with each nod or critique. This dependence can leave you vulnerable, as the validation you seek becomes a double-edged sword, offering temporary relief while reinforcing the belief that your value lies outside yourself. The quest for approval becomes a cycle, where each external affirmation temporarily masks the internal void but never truly fills it. This can lead to a constant seeking, a restless pursuit of praise and acceptance that never quite satisfies.

Shifting from a reliance on external validation to cultivating self-acceptance is a transformative process, one that requires introspection and intention. Start by incorporating positive self-affirmations into your daily routine. These affirmations are powerful tools, simple statements that remind you of your inherent worth and capabilities. By repeating them regularly, you begin to internalize their truths, slowly reshaping the narrative you hold about yourself. Practicing gratitude is another cornerstone of self-acceptance. By focusing on the positive aspects of your life and the qualities you appreciate in yourself, you nurture a sense of contentment and fulfillment that is independent of external approval. Gratitude helps reframe your perspective, allowing you to see the abundance in your life rather than the perceived lack.

The pathway to self-love is ongoing, a continuous unfolding that invites you to explore the depths of who you are. Consider creating a self-love journal, a dedicated space where you can document your thoughts, feelings, and insights. Use this journal to reflect on your daily experiences, noting moments of self-appreciation and gratitude. This practice reinforces self-acceptance and serves as a tangible reminder of your growth and resilience. Regular self-reflection is equally important, offering a chance to pause and consider the progress you've made. Take time to acknowledge your achievements, both big and small, and the ways in which you've handled challenges. This reflection creates a deeper understanding of yourself, allowing you to embrace your unique journey with compassion and grace. As you develop self-love, you begin to realize that your worth is not contingent on external factors, like your unavailable, absent father, but is intrinsic and unwavering.

Setting Boundaries: Protecting Your Emotional Well-being

Imagine your personal space as a garden, one where the plants need careful tending to flourish. Boundaries act as the fence around this garden, protecting your emotional well-being from the intrusive weeds of overbearing influences and expectations. Healthy boundaries are essential to relationships, serving as markers that define the limits between you and others. They can be emotional, safeguarding your feelings and thoughts, or physical, delineating the personal space you need to feel safe. These boundaries are necessary for maintaining a sense of self-respect and integrity, allowing you to interact with others without losing sight of your individual needs and values. They ensure that your garden remains a sanctuary, a place where you can nurture your well-being while engaging meaningfully with the world around you.

Establishing boundaries can be particularly challenging for those who have grown up without a father. The absence of a paternal figure might have led to a heightened fear of rejection, making it difficult to assert your needs or say "no" without guilt. This fear often stems from early experiences where love and acceptance felt conditional, dependent on compliance and sacrifice. Without a model for healthy boundary-setting, you might find yourself accommodating others at the expense of your own needs, trapped in patterns where your desires are sidelined to avoid conflict or disapproval. The apprehension of being abandoned or unloved if you assert yourself can be a powerful deterrent, leaving you vulnerable to the encroachments of others who may not have your best interests at heart.

However, learning to set and maintain healthy boundaries is a skill that can be developed with practice and intention. Assertiveness training can be immensely beneficial, giving you the tools to communicate your needs clearly and confidently. This involves expressing your thoughts and feelings in a direct yet respectful manner, ensuring that your voice is heard without infringing on the rights of others. Practicing saying "no" is another important aspect, as it reinforces your autonomy and the legitimacy of your boundaries. Start small, perhaps by declining minor requests that don't align with your priorities, gradually building the courage to assert yourself in more significant situations. Each time you practice setting a boundary, you strengthen the fence around your garden, safeguarding the space that nurtures your growth and well-being.

The positive impacts of boundary-setting on emotional health are profound. By establishing clear limits, you cultivate increased self-respect, recognizing and valuing your worth as an individual. This self-respect translates into healthier relationships, where interactions are based on mutual understanding and respect rather than obligation or resentment. Boundaries empower you to engage with others from a place of strength and clarity, where your needs are acknowledged and your individuality is honored. They create a foundation of trust and integrity, allowing you to form connections that are both supportive and enriching. In protecting your emotional well-being, boundaries serve as the pillars that uphold your sense of self, enabling you to navigate relationships with confidence and grace.

As you explore the role of boundaries in your life, consider how they can transform your interactions, offering a balance between connection and independence. The journey to understanding and establishing boundaries is ongoing, a testament to your commitment to personal growth and emotional health. By embracing the power of boundaries, you take a vital step toward creating a life that reflects your values and supports your well-being. As you continue to explore these themes, remember that each boundary you set is a declaration of self-respect, a commitment to nurturing the garden of your life.

In the next chapter, we will further explore the dynamics of relationships, focusing on the influence of early experiences on your interactions and emotional health. Through understanding, you can continue to build a life filled with meaningful connections and personal fulfillment.

Chapter 7

Growing up without a father can cast a long shadow on how you experience love and intimacy in your adult life. As a daughter of an absent father, romantic relationships often feel like a confusing and uncertain path, shaped by the absence of paternal guidance. Without realizing it, you may find yourself repeatedly drawn to emotionally unavailable partners, unconsciously seeking to recreate the emotional distance you experienced as a child. This pattern isn't about making poor choices; it's a subconscious attempt to resolve the void left by your father's absence, hoping that by fixing this dynamic, you can finally heal.

In relationships, this dynamic often shows up as a tendency to prioritize your partner's needs above your own. You may take on the role of the caregiver, the one who listens, supports, and gives, often at the cost of your own boundaries and desires. This pattern can be rooted in the belief that you do not deserve love and must attempt to win it through sacrifice and selflessness. You may feel validated only when you're giving, mirroring the roles you assumed in your family to try and fill the emotional gap left by your father. Over time, this self-sacrifice can leave you emotionally depleted, questioning whether you are enough or deserving of love simply as you are.

These patterns also affect your ability to form deep emotional intimacy. As a daughter of an absent father, the fear of vulnerability and rejection can make it difficult to express your true feelings. You may keep your emotions guarded, fearing that opening up could lead to the same abandonment you experienced growing up. The walls you've built to protect yourself may keep others at a distance, preventing genuine connection and creating a sense of isolation even in the presence of a partner. This emotional detachment, though protective, can make relationships feel shallow and unfulfilling.

Breaking free from these harmful patterns requires intentional effort and self-awareness. Start by recognizing the red flags that indicate unhealthy dynamics. Reflect on what you truly need and deserve in a relationship, and set clear boundaries that honor your worth. Self-reflection can help you uncover the underlying fears and needs that have shaped your behavior, allowing you to regain control over your relationship choices. Understanding why you might prioritize others' needs over your own is key to reclaiming your agency and choosing healthier, more fulfilling connections.

Building emotional intimacy requires intentional steps. Practice active listening and empathy in your conversations, focusing on responding and truly understanding your partner. This creates space for both of you to feel heard and valued. Additionally, shared experiences, whether through regular date nights, cooking together, or enjoying a common hobby, can help strengthen your bond. These rituals provide continuity and a sense of connection, reminding you of your emotional connection. By taking these steps, you can begin to break the cycle and build the deep, fulfilling relationships you deserve.

Redefining Relationship Patterns

Take a moment to reflect on your romantic relationships, past and present. Consider the following questions:

- What patterns do you notice in your choice of partners and relationship dynamics?

- How do you prioritize your needs alongside those of your partner?

- What fears or beliefs might be influencing these patterns, and how can you address them?

By exploring these questions, you can gain insights into your relationship patterns and make conscious choices supporting healthier dynamics. This reflection is not about assigning blame but understanding the influences shaping your journey. As you engage with this process, remember that change is possible and that every step toward self-awareness brings you closer to the fulfilling relationships you deserve.

Unhealthy Relationship Patterns

Daughters who grow up without a father often lack a positive relationship model to base their romantic relationships. A father's influence shapes a daughter's understanding of love, respect, and healthy boundaries within relationships. Without this foundational model, many daughters may struggle to understand what a balanced, supportive partnership looks like. They may not fully recognize what it means to be treated with the care and respect they deserve because they were never shown these examples firsthand. This absence leaves them searching for validation and connection, often in the wrong places.

Without a father figure, daughters may unconsciously seek relationships that mirror the emotional distance or neglect they experienced growing up. Without realizing it, they may gravitate toward partners who are emotionally unavailable, distant, or unable to meet their emotional needs. This tendency is not a sign of poor judgment but rather an attempt to recreate the emotional dynamics they are familiar with. Unfortunately, these relationships are often unhealthy, leaving them feeling unfulfilled, undervalued, and trapped in a cycle of disappointment. They may internalize the belief that this is what love is supposed to feel like, leading them to accept far less than they deserve.

Because they haven't been shown what a healthy, loving partnership looks like, daughters without a father figure may struggle to establish clear boundaries in their romantic relationships. They might find themselves prioritizing their partner's needs over their own, hoping that by giving more of themselves, they will receive the love and attention they've longed for. This often leads to an imbalance, where they sacrifice their happiness, identity, and well-being to keep the relationship intact. Over time, this self-sacrifice erodes their self-worth, and they may begin to feel as though their needs don't matter or that they are undeserving of a relationship where they are treated with respect and love.

The lack of a positive relationship model often keeps daughters from recognizing the signs of an unhealthy dynamic. They may feel trapped in relationships where they give endlessly but receive little in return, unsure how to break free from the cycle. This repeated pattern of unhealthy relationships can create deep emotional wounds, leading to feelings of inadequacy, loneliness, and a lack of confidence in their ability to form fulfilling connections. Healing these wounds requires understanding the root of these patterns, learning to set healthy boundaries, and recognizing their worth in relationships. Only then can they begin to break free from the cycle of unhealthy partnerships and find the love they truly deserve.

Setting Boundaries with Confidence

Imagine a world where your personal space is a fortress, not to shut others out but to protect your peace and well-being. Boundaries are the invisible lines that define where you end and others begin, necessary for maintaining healthy relationships and safeguarding emotional health. They act as a framework for how you allow others to treat you and how you treat yourself, ensuring that your needs are respected and understood. Healthy boundaries are flexible, adapting as relationships evolve, while unhealthy ones can be too rigid or too porous, leading to control issues or feelings of vulnerability. Recognizing when these lines are crossed is very important. Signs of boundary violations might include feeling drained after interactions, being resentful for unmet needs, or living in fear of conflict. These signals are your mind's way of alerting you that your boundaries need attention.

Setting boundaries can be daunting, especially if you grew up without a paternal figure to model them. The fear of rejection or conflict often looms large, whispering that asserting your needs may push loved ones away. Internalized beliefs about self-worth, shaped by early experiences, can further complicate this process. You might worry that setting boundaries makes you demanding or selfish or fear that doing so will drive a wedge between you and those you care about. These fears often originate from wanting to be accepted and loved, a desire to keep the peace at the expense of your own comfort. But setting boundaries isn't about creating distance but building respect for yourself and others.

To set effective boundaries, start with clear and assertive communication. This means expressing your needs honestly and directly, using "I" statements to articulate your feelings and needs. For example, instead of saying, "You never listen to me," try, "I feel unheard when my thoughts aren't considered." This approach focuses on your experience rather than placing blame, reducing defensiveness, and opening the door to constructive dialogue. Practicing self-care becomes an act of reinforcing these boundaries, ensuring that you maintain the energy and clarity needed to uphold them. Self-care can be as simple as taking time to rest, pursuing hobbies, or seeking solitude when needed. By prioritizing your well-being, you strengthen your ability to communicate and enforce your boundaries.

Conflicts may arise when boundaries are asserted, but they can be handled with respect and patience. Negotiating compromises involves finding a middle ground where both parties feel heard and valued. It's about balancing your needs with those of others, ensuring that solutions are mutually beneficial. Seek support from trusted mentors or therapists who can offer guidance and perspective. They can help you explore the roots of your boundary challenges and provide strategies for maintaining them. Therapy, particularly for those grappling with the effects of absent fathers, can be transformative. It offers a safe space to practice boundary-setting skills and gain confidence in your ability to uphold them.

Boundary-Setting Practice

Consider engaging in a boundary-setting exercise to explore this concept further. Think about an area in your life where boundaries feel blurry or non-existent. Reflect on the following questions:

- What specific boundaries do you need in this area, and why?

- How can you communicate these boundaries clearly and assertively?

- What language will you use to express your needs?

- What self-care practices can support you in maintaining these boundaries?

By taking the time to explore and articulate your boundary needs, you empower yourself to create relationships that honor and respect your individuality. Remember, boundaries create a space where trust and respect can flourish. They are the foundation upon which healthy, fulfilling relationships are built, allowing you to engage with the world confidently and authentically.

Cultivating Trust: A New Foundation

Imagine trying to build a house on shaky ground. That's what relationships can feel like when trust is absent. Trust is the bedrock of any meaningful connection. Without it, relationships can crumble under the weight of doubt and suspicion. Trust can be a particularly fragile construct for those who have experienced the absence of a father. Early experiences might have taught you that people can leave, promises can be broken, and love can be conditional. Rebuilding trust requires acknowledging these personal barriers, understanding their origins, and committing to a process of healing and growth. Recognizing that trust is foundational means accepting that it underpins your interactions, shaping how you perceive and respond to others. It's about acknowledging that what was once lost can be rebuilt, stronger, and more resilient than before.

To cultivate trust, honesty and transparency must become your companions. This means being open about your feelings and intentions, even when vulnerability feels daunting. Practice articulating your truth clearly in conversations, allowing others to see your genuine self. This honesty encourages reciprocal openness, creating a space where mutual understanding can flourish. Share your personal stories and experiences, not as a means of seeking sympathy but as a way to build bridges of empathy and connection. These stories can be windows into your world, offering insight into the values and experiences that shape your perspective. By inviting others into your narrative, you lay the groundwork for relationships built on authenticity and respect.

Handling the challenges of trust-building is no small feat. Setbacks are inevitable, as trust is sometimes tested. When breaches occur, it's crucial to approach the situation with patience and empathy. This doesn't mean ignoring the hurt or glossing over the breach but acknowledging the impact and taking steps to address it. Rebuilding after a breach involves honest dialogue, where both parties express their feelings and work toward understanding and resolution. Developing patience means recognizing that trust is not rebuilt overnight; it requires consistent, intentional effort and a willingness to forgive. Empathy lets you understand the other person's perspective, promoting compassion and a shared commitment to moving forward. This rebuilding process can be a deepening experience, challenging you to confront discomfort and embrace growth.

Cultivating self-trust is an integral part of the trust-building process. Without it, trusting others can feel like walking on a tightrope without a safety net. Self-trust involves engaging in self-reflective practices that enhance self-awareness. By understanding your thoughts, emotions, and reactions, you create a dialogue with yourself that paves the way for confidence and clarity. Recognize and honor your personal values and instincts, as they serve as your internal compass, guiding your decisions and interactions. Trusting yourself means believing in your ability to manage challenges, make choices that align with your true self, and learn from experiences. It's about embracing your strengths and acknowledging your vulnerabilities, understanding that both are part of what makes you whole.

Building Self-Trust

Think about a moment when you felt uncertain or doubted your instincts. Reflect on the following questions:

- What did you learn about yourself from that experience?

- How can you honor your values and instincts moving forward?

- In what ways can you cultivate self-trust in your daily life?

By engaging in this exercise, you can begin to strengthen your relationship with yourself, laying the foundation for trusting others. As you cultivate this inner trust, your capacity to build and nurture trusting relationships expands, creating connections that are rich with understanding and support.

Dynamics in Friendships

Friendships can be especially challenging for those who grew up without a father. Without a paternal figure to model loyalty and commitment, it can be difficult to understand what true friendship really means. The absence of a father often creates a lingering fear that others, like a father, could leave unexpectedly. This fear of abandonment can make you more likely to over-give in relationships, hoping that you'll secure a sense of belonging and emotional security by being there for others.

This fear of losing friends can lead to clinging too tightly, which may unintentionally push them away. When your happiness and sense of self-worth depend on the approval or presence of others, it can create feelings of jealousy, comparison, and competition. You might find yourself questioning whether the success or happiness of your friends diminishes your own, which strains relationships and creates unnecessary tension. The imbalance of giving more than you receive can lead to emotional exhaustion, as you are expending more energy than you are getting in return. Over time, this imbalance can result in resentment, undermining the foundation of trust and mutual respect essential for healthy, lasting friendships.

To encourage healthy and fulfilling friendships, it's important to set mutual expectations and boundaries. Clear communication about what you need from a friendship and understanding what your friends need in return creates a framework for respect and support. Engage in activities that nurture shared interests, offering opportunities to bond over common passions. Whether it's a shared love of hiking, book clubs, or cooking, these activities provide a connection, allowing friendships to flourish naturally. By participating in activities you both enjoy, you create memories that reinforce the ties that bind you, strengthening your connection through shared experiences. These moments of joy and laughter become the foundation of your friendship, creating a bond rich with understanding and care.

Developing a supportive network of friends requires effort and intentionality, where connection and mutual growth are the key outcomes. Seek friendships that align with your values, as these are the ones that will resonate most deeply with your sense of self. Surround yourself with individuals who uplift and inspire you and who challenge you to grow while accepting you as you are. Engaging in community groups, clubs, and volunteering can help broaden your social circles, connecting you with like-minded individuals who share your interests and ideals. These spaces provide opportunities for meaningful interactions and new connections, each with the potential to evolve into lasting friendships. As you build this network, remember that nurturing each relationship with care and attention is crucial, as friendships, like all important aspects of life, require effort and commitment to thrive.

The absence of a father can shape how you perceive and engage with others, particularly in your friendships. However, with awareness and intention, you can create meaningful and fulfilling relationships, offering support and joy through life's challenges. Friendships celebrate connections that enrich your life, not just fill a void. As you continue to build these bonds, you create a supportive community that reflects the love and loyalty you deserve. Your friendships become a testament to your resilience and ability to connect with others, a reminder that you are never truly alone even in the face of absence.

As we close this chapter, remember that friendships are a vital part of your life. They provide support, joy, and understanding, helping you face the challenges and triumphs of your journey. In the next chapter, we will explore how these relationships connect with other aspects of your life, shaping your sense of self and belonging.

Chapter 8

G rowing up without a father can leave a deep, lingering void that impacts your sense of self. Without a paternal figure to help guide your development and shape your understanding of relationships, you may ask, "Who am I without my father?" This question can feel daunting and overwhelming, but it is important. The absence of a father can influence how you view yourself, your self-worth, and the way you relate to others. However, in confronting this absence, there is also an opportunity for profound self-discovery, where you can define your identity on your own terms, independent of any missing influence.

The process of discovering who you truly are requires introspection and honesty. It begins with examining your core values and beliefs, the guiding principles that shape your thoughts, actions, and decisions. Reflect on what truly matters to you and what gives you meaning and purpose in life. Consider what stirs your passions and gives you energy. This reflection will help you understand your deeper motivations and desires. Recognizing your values establishes a foundation for living authentically, grounded in what resonates most deeply with you. This also includes identifying your unique talents and passions, whether it's a sport, music, helping others, or pursuing a specific career. These activities bring you joy and fulfillment and are integral to your identity, giving you a clearer picture of who you are and want to become.

The absence of a father likely shapes many aspects of your identity, from how you relate to others to how you approach challenges. Without a father to model healthy relationships, knowing what loyalty, commitment, and love truly look like can be difficult. You might wrestle with the impact of his absence, wondering how it has affected your self-perception or questioning if you have inherited any traits from him. It's easy to fixate on what you didn't have, but it's equally important to consider the other role models who have stepped in to fill that space. Teachers, mentors, coaches, family members, and close friends can offer valuable guidance and support, teaching you resilience, independence, and empathy lessons. Though not a father, these figures have influenced your development in meaningful ways. They've helped shape your worldview, often providing insights that have enabled you to thrive despite the absence of your father's presence. By acknowledging the impact of these people, you can recognize the diversity of relationships that have contributed to your growth.

Building self-awareness is essential to understanding your identity, especially if you grew up without a father. Self-reflection allows you to look closer at your thoughts, emotions, and behaviors, helping you uncover patterns in your relationships and personal choices. Journaling can be a useful tool in this process. Writing down your experiences, reflections, and insights can help you organize your thoughts and identify recurring themes in your life. Over time, you'll notice certain tendencies; perhaps you over-give in relationships, or maybe you struggle to trust others. These revelations give you the power to make conscious changes. In addition to journaling, you might also consider using personality assessments such as the Enneagram, Myers-Briggs, or StrengthsFinder. These tools can offer a structured approach to understanding your inherent traits and preferences, helping you gain deeper insight into who you are and how you engage with the world. They can be a mirror, reflecting aspects of yourself you may not have fully recognized.

Another critical aspect of forming your identity, especially as someone who grew up without a father, is learning to embrace independence. This means developing decision-making skills that allow you to trust your judgment and handle life's uncertainties with confidence. Not having a father in your life negatively affects your self-confidence. To build your self-confidence, it is important to stand on your own two feet and trust that you are capable of making choices that are right for you. Start by making small decisions that align with your values and passions. Every time you choose to do something based on what feels true to you, you strengthen your sense of agency and autonomy. Over time, making decisions becomes easier, and you'll feel more empowered to pursue your larger dreams. Whether you want to explore new career opportunities, take up a new hobby, or challenge yourself in ways you never have before, these pursuits allow you to expand your sense of possibility. Your independence becomes a foundation for building confidence and self-assurance, allowing you to live more fully as the person you are becoming.

While the absence of a father figure undoubtedly shapes many parts of your life, it also provides the space for you to define your own identity. By engaging in deep self-reflection, recognizing the role of other important figures in your life, and embracing your independence, you create the opportunity to shape who you are, independent of your past. This exploration of self-discovery and self-empowerment is essential to living authentically and confidently, allowing you to build the future that aligns with your true self.

Discovering Your Unique Identity

Take a quiet moment to engage in this reflection exercise. With a notebook and pen, find a comfortable space where you can reflect without interruption. Consider these questions:

- What are my core values, and how do they guide my choices?

- Who are the role models that have influenced my growth, and what have they taught me?

- Even though my father was not in my life, who stepped in and helped guide, teach, and support me?

- What are my unique talents and passions, and how can I nurture them?

As you write, allow yourself to explore your thoughts and emotions without judgment. This exercise is a step toward embracing the fullness of your identity and acknowledging the myriad influences that have shaped you. Understanding who you are without your father creates space for growth and self-discovery, building a foundation for a future defined by authenticity and purpose.

Redefining Self-Identity: Beyond the Absence

There comes a time when you must redefine who you are beyond the shadow of your father's absence. This process involves examining the limiting beliefs that have taken root over the years. Like tangled vines, these beliefs can restrict your view of yourself and your potential. Perhaps you've internalized the notion that you are somehow less than, simply because a father's presence was missing. Challenge these assumptions. Ask yourself where they originated and why they persist.

By questioning them, you loosen their grip, allowing space for a more authentic and empowered self-identity to emerge. Reclaiming your narrative means taking control of the stories you tell about yourself. It involves acknowledging the painful parts yet recognizing that they do not define you entirely. Consider the moments of strength and resilience that punctuate your story. These are building blocks for your new narrative that highlight your courage and adaptability. This narrative is yours to craft, free from the constraints of what might have been.

Resilience plays a pivotal role in transforming self-identity. It is the ability to learn from past experiences and mistakes, using them as stepping stones rather than stumbling blocks. Reflect on the times you've faced adversity and found a way through. Each of these moments contributes to your reservoir of strength. Embrace the lessons they offer. Adopting a growth mindset opens you to the possibility of change and development. This mindset encourages you to view challenges as growth opportunities rather than insurmountable obstacles. It empowers you to see yourself not as a static being but as someone capable of evolution and transformation. Crafting a new self-narrative requires intentionality and creativity. Begin by writing affirmations that reflect the person you are becoming. These affirmations serve as powerful reminders of your growth and potential. Consider visualizing your future self through guided imagery, imagining the life you wish to lead and the qualities you aim to embody. This exercise can be incredibly motivating, providing a clear vision of who you are striving to become.

Integrating past experiences with present aspirations is important in shaping your identity. Reflect on pivotal life moments that have influenced you. What have they taught you about yourself and your values? Use these reflections as a foundation upon which to build your future. Set intentions for personal development that align with your newfound understanding of who you are. These intentions will guide you toward a life that is fulfilling and true to your core. As you embrace this process, remember that identity is not a fixed construct. It is a dynamic and evolving aspect of your being, one that can be continually reshaped and refined.

Visualization Exercise: Crafting Your Future Self

Take a moment to close your eyes and visualize your future self. Picture the life you wish to lead, the qualities you aim to embody, and the impact you hope to have on those around you. As you do this, focus on the emotions and sensations that arise. Write down your vision, capturing the essence of your future self in words. This exercise is a powerful tool for motivation and clarity, helping you align your actions with your aspirations.

Embracing this journey of self-discovery is an act of courage. It involves letting go of old narratives that no longer serve you and stepping into a new chapter with confidence and intention. Your father's absence may have shaped certain aspects of your identity, but it does not define you. You have the power to redefine who you are, to craft a self-identity that is rich with possibility and grounded in authenticity. As you move forward, trust in your ability to navigate the complexities of identity transformation, knowing that each step brings you closer to the self you are meant to be.

Embracing Cultural and Personal Diversity

Many cultures place a strong emphasis on the traditional family model, where a father is present and plays an active role in a child's life.

Growing up without a father, you may have felt like an outsider, uncomfortable in spaces where the typical family structure was the norm. These cultural expectations can make you feel as though you don't fit in or that something is missing, even if you were surrounded by love and care in other forms.

However, it's important to shed these feelings of inadequacy and understand that your family dynamic doesn't define your worth. The absence of a father doesn't diminish your value or the love you've received from other sources. Recognizing that you belong exactly as you are and that your experiences, even without a traditional father figure, are valid can help you embrace your true self. Your identity is shaped by much more than the family structure you're part of, it's shaped by your strength, resilience, and ability to create meaningful connections in your own way.

Creating a Vision for Your Future

Take a moment to reflect on where you are in your life and where you want to go. Growing and shaping your future starts with understanding your personal goals, both short-term and long-term. These goals are the foundation of your journey, guiding you toward the life you want to create. Short-term goals, like learning a new skill or developing a daily habit, provide immediate focus and a sense of accomplishment. Long-term goals, such as pursuing a career change or launching a personal project, give you a broader direction, ensuring that your actions align with your deeper values and aspirations.

Once you've identified your goals, it's important to break them down into actionable steps. This is where strategic planning comes into play. By developing a plan, you can map out the path ahead and make your goals more attainable. Think of each step as a task that brings you closer to your desired outcome. You must also consider any obstacles that might arise along the way and plan how to handle them. For example, if you want to advance in your career, assess the skills you need and seek opportunities to acquire them. If financial constraints are an issue, explore alternatives like scholarships or part-time work. Having a clear plan helps you stay focused and resilient in the face of challenges.

Motivation and perseverance are key to keeping your vision alive. Reflect on why each goal matters to you, and how it aligns with your sense of purpose. When motivation begins to wane, revisit your reasons for pursuing these goals. Building resilience is equally important, setbacks will happen, but they offer valuable learning experiences. Instead of seeing failure as a roadblock, view it as an opportunity to improve and adapt. Resilience isn't about avoiding challenges but about pushing forward and growing stronger each time you face them.

Personal growth is a lifelong journey, and embracing learning is at the heart of this process. Seek out opportunities that expand your knowledge and skills, whether through formal education, workshops, or self-guided exploration. Being open to new experiences helps you grow, both personally and professionally. Each new skill you acquire and every challenge you overcome adds richness to your life and broadens your perspective. The more you learn, the more you develop an understanding of who you are and what you're capable of achieving.

By identifying your goals, creating a strategic plan, and committing to growth, you are shaping the future you want to live. The absence of a father may have influenced your past, but it does not have to affect your future. With each step forward, you can create a life of purpose, fulfillment, and joy.

Chapter 9

In the quiet moments before dawn, when the mind is free, you may find yourself reflecting on thoughts tied to an absent father. Journaling can help you process these feelings, offering a private space to express emotions without judgment. By putting your thoughts on paper, you can gain insight into your inner world and understand how your experiences have shaped you.

Journaling enhances self-awareness by encouraging reflection. It provides a safe space to explore vulnerable feelings and examine your experiences. This process helps you connect with yourself, cultivating empathy and clarity. Through journaling, you begin to understand your emotional trauma and the patterns that influence your behavior.

Different journaling techniques can deepen your emotional exploration. Stream-of-consciousness writing allows you to express raw, unfiltered thoughts, revealing hidden emotions. Gratitude journaling shifts your focus to positive aspects of life, fostering resilience. Prompt-based journaling provides structure, guiding you to specific areas of reflection and growth.

Creating a journaling habit can offer stability and routine. Set aside time each day, whether in the morning or evening, to reflect and write. Personalizing your journal with meaningful items or quotes can make the practice more meaningful. Journaling supports emotional exploration and provides clarity and insights into challenges, helping you find solutions and new perspectives.

Journaling Prompts for Self-Discovery

Consider using the following prompts to guide your journaling practice and deepen your self-discovery:

1. What emotions arise when you think about your father's absence, and how do they manifest in your life?

2. In what ways have you grown or changed as a result of dealing with this experience?

3. What are three things challenging?

These questions can help you reflect on your experiences, providing valuable insights into how your father's absence has shaped your emotions and growth. Journaling is a personal practice, and as you explore these prompts, remember there are no right or wrong answers, only your unique truth waiting to be uncovered.

Gratitude Journaling for Healing

Gratitude journaling can be a powerful tool for shifting your focus from pain to appreciation, particularly when healing from the absence of a father. It can help you recognize the positive aspects of your life, even under challenging circumstances. Reflecting on gratitude builds resilience and allows you to reconnect with what truly matters.

As a daughter growing up without a father, ask yourself these three questions to guide your gratitude practice:

1. What qualities or strengths have I developed from facing life

without my father?

2. How have other positive relationships, such as with a mentor or a close friend, enriched my life?

3. What moments, big or small, today made me feel supported, loved, or valued?

These questions can help you shift your focus to the blessings and strengths you've cultivated, even in the face of hardship. Regularly practicing gratitude can uncover moments of healing and self-growth that may have gone unnoticed. Gratitude journaling is an opportunity to acknowledge your positive impact in your own life despite the absence of a father.

Developing a Self-Care Routine

Self-care might sound like a luxury, something reserved for those with ample time and resources. Yet, it's a vital part of maintaining both emotional and physical well-being, especially for those who grew up carrying the weight of an absent father. Self-care is not just about pampering oneself; it's the foundation for resilience and recovery. It's about preserving your mental health and ensuring that the demands of life don't lead to burnout. Caring for yourself creates a buffer against the stresses that threaten balance, nurturing a space where healing can occur. This practice provides the strength to face life's challenges with grace and determination, acting as a cornerstone for rebuilding and maintaining a sense of equilibrium.

A personalized self-care routine can include various components, each tailored to your unique needs and preferences. Physical activities like yoga or walking offer more than just fitness benefits; they connect your body and mind, grounding you in the present moment. These activities can be a form of moving meditation, allowing you to release tension and find peace within your physical space. Mental relaxation techniques such as meditation or deep breathing exercises provide a retreat for your mind, a way to quiet the chaos and find clarity amidst the noise. Creative outlets like painting or music allow you to express emotions that might be difficult to articulate, offering a release and a way to process feelings in a tangible form.

Tailoring your self-care routine means identifying activities that bring joy and relaxation, resonate with your soul, and provide genuine comfort. It's about listening to your inner voice and recognizing what truly nourishes you rather than adhering to societal norms or expectations. Adaptability is important, as your needs may change over time or in response to life's fluctuations. What worked yesterday may not work today, and that's okay. Embrace the fluidity of your routine, allowing it to evolve with you. This flexibility ensures that self-care remains a nurturing practice rather than a rigid obligation, creating a sense of well-being that aligns with your current state.

However, maintaining a consistent self-care routine can be challenging, especially when life feels overwhelming. It's easy to prioritize everything else and place self-care on the back burner. Setting realistic expectations and goals can help overcome these barriers, ensuring that self-care becomes an integral part of your daily life rather than an afterthought. Start small, incorporating manageable practices that fit into your schedule, even if it's just a few minutes of meditation or a short walk. Remember, self-care is not about perfection; it's about progress and intention. Prioritize these moments, recognizing their value amidst the demands of your day.

In the hustle and bustle of daily life, it can be difficult to find time for self-care. Busy schedules, responsibilities and external pressures often take precedence, leaving little room for personal well-being. To combat this, consider integrating self-care into your routine rather than viewing it as an additional task. Perhaps it's enjoying a quiet cup of tea in the morning, taking a few deep breaths before a meeting, or listening to your favorite music during your commute. These small, intentional moments can make a significant difference, reminding you to pause, breathe, and reconnect with yourself. By incorporating self-care into your life, you ensure that it becomes a sustainable and enriching practice that supports your overall well-being and fosters resilience.

Mindfulness Practices for Daily Life

Imagine starting each day with a moment of stillness, where the breath flows effortlessly and time seems to pause. This is the essence of mindfulness, which invites you to fully inhabit the present moment. Integrating mindfulness into your daily routine need not be daunting; it can be as simple as incorporating mindful breathing during everyday activities. As you go about your day, whether driving to work or waiting in line, focus on your breath. Notice its rhythm, the way it fills your lungs and then gently releases. This practice helps anchor you in the here and now, bringing a sense of calm and presence to even the most mundane tasks. Consider practicing mindfulness during routine activities like eating or cleaning. When you're eating, savor each bite, paying attention to the flavors and textures. When cleaning, focus on the motions of your hands and the sensations they create. These small acts of mindfulness transform ordinary moments into opportunities for connection with yourself, creating a sense of peace and clarity.

In times of stress, specific mindfulness techniques can provide relief and promote relaxation. Body scan meditation is a powerful tool for releasing tension. As you lie quietly, intentionally guide your awareness through each part of your body, noticing areas of tightness and consciously letting them go. This meditative practice soothes the nervous system and enhances your connection with your physical self, creating an awareness that carries into other aspects of life. Guided imagery, on the other hand, involves visualizing calming scenes or experiences, such as walking through a peaceful forest or lying on a sunlit beach. This technique encourages your mind to escape the chaos of daily life, offering a mental sanctuary where stress can dissolve. Dedicating even a few minutes to these practices creates a refuge for your mind and body, nurturing a sense of balance and well-being.

Creating mindful moments throughout the day can be transformative, cultivating awareness and gratitude. Consider setting digital reminders to pause and breathe, allowing yourself to step back and reset your mind. These reminders act as gentle prompts, inviting you to return to the present amidst the hustle and bustle of your schedule. Engage in short, mindful pauses between tasks, taking a few deep breaths and centering yourself before moving on. This approach enhances focus and productivity and reduces the likelihood of feeling overwhelmed. By scheduling moments of mindfulness into your day, you cultivate a habit of presence and awareness that becomes second nature. These mindful interludes create space for reflection and appreciation, giving you a sense of gratitude for the small joys and experiences that often go unnoticed.

Adopting a mindful mindset has far-reaching benefits, particularly in enhancing emotional resilience. By training your mind to stay present in challenging situations, you develop the ability to respond thoughtfully rather than react impulsively. This heightened awareness allows you to observe your emotions without judgment, giving you a deeper understanding of your emotional state. Improved emotional regulation becomes possible as you gain insight into the patterns and triggers influencing your responses. With practice, you begin to approach life's challenges calmly and clearly, confident in your ability to respond to whatever arises. Mindfulness becomes a guiding force, helping you remain grounded and centered even amidst life's storms. As you cultivate this mindset, you discover a profound sense of connection with yourself and the world around you, embracing each moment with openness and curiosity.

Building Emotional Resilience

Emotional resilience is the ability to recover from setbacks and adversity. It doesn't mean avoiding pain but having the strength to face challenges and grow stronger from them. Resilience is about being proactive in maintaining emotional health and learning to handle difficulties without waiting for them to pass.

To build resilience, start with positive self-talk. Reframe negative thoughts, like replacing "I'm not good enough" with "I'm learning and growing." This shift can help you approach challenges with confidence. Engaging in problem-solving exercises also strengthens resilience by encouraging creative and adaptable thinking. Pushing yourself out of your comfort zone, such as by trying new experiences, builds confidence and prepares you for unexpected situations.

Social support plays a crucial role in resilience. Building a network of supportive people provides emotional strength during tough times. Engaging with community groups or activities can expand your support system, offering connection and understanding from others who share similar experiences.

Maintaining resilience requires commitment. Set personal goals that challenge you, and regularly review them to track your progress.

Reflecting on past challenges and how you overcame them can reinforce your belief in your resilience. Remember, resilience is a continuous process. It's about embracing your journey, learning from challenges, and trusting in your ability to overcome whatever comes your way.

Celebrating Small Victories in Healing

In moments of reflection, it's easy to overlook the small victories along your path to healing. Yet, these milestones are essential for progress, no matter how minor. Recognizing personal growth means noticing shifts in perspective, where you begin to see the world and yourself differently. Each breakthrough, whether it's responding with calm or expressing an emotion you once suppressed, is a victory. Healing is not just about the end result; it's about celebrating each step forward, even if small.

Create rituals to honor these changes, reinforcing them as milestones that ground you in the present. Consider keeping a success diary, where you document each achievement, regardless of size. Whether it's a day when you felt lighter, a moment of self-care, or a time you stood up for yourself, writing these down helps solidify your progress. Such practices help you focus on your accomplishments rather than what's left to do. Reward yourself with small treats or meaningful experiences as a reminder that even small steps are worth celebrating.

Celebrating small victories is a powerful motivator, helping to sustain your momentum for healing. Each acknowledgment boosts your confidence and reinforces your belief in your ability to overcome challenges. Positive reinforcement encourages persistence, even when progress feels slow. By celebrating, you affirm your strength and re-

silience, reminding yourself of your capabilities. The more you celebrate, the more you build self-belief and keep pushing forward, fueling
your progress. Eventually, it will become its own self-reinforcing cycle.

Building a culture of celebration extends beyond personal recognition; it invites others to share in your victories. Share your successes
with supportive friends or groups to amplify the joy and create a sense
of community around your healing. When you openly recognize and
celebrate your achievements, you encourage others to do the same,
creating a ripple effect of positivity. This shared celebration strengthens your bonds and creates a network of support where mutual inspiration helps everyone grow. As you continue to heal, remember these
small victories are not just something to be proud of but reminders of
your resilience and strength.

Chapter 10

In moments of reflection, especially for daughters who grew up without a father, it's easy to question the value of another self-help book. With so many options available, skepticism is natural. What makes this book different? This isn't just another generic guide; it's specifically designed to address the emotional challenges that arise from a father's absence. It's a companion that understands the impact of growing up without a father and offers both relatable insights and practical strategies tailored to your experience.

The stories in this book mirror your struggles, providing both validation and hope. They showcase resilience and growth, demonstrating how others have worked through similar pain. These narratives provide a roadmap to healing, offering tangible examples of how to move forward. Alongside these stories, the book introduces therapeutic techniques, like mindfulness and cognitive-behavioral strategies, grounded in real-world application. These tools are designed to fit into your daily life, providing you with a clear, practical way to heal and grow.

Unlike many self-help books that promise change without delivering, this one is focused on what really works. It understands that healing is personal and requires actionable steps. Each chapter offers expert guidance, but more importantly, it provides exercises and journaling prompts that encourage active participation. You're not just reading—you're engaging, making this book a useful tool for personal growth, complementing therapy, and allowing you to apply what you learn in your everyday life.

The real transformation happens when you engage actively with the content. Passive reading won't bring the change you're looking for. You'll see the greatest benefit through journaling, reflecting, and setting goals. Each chapter encourages you to take ownership of your healing, track your progress, and celebrate the small victories. This approach will build your confidence and help you move through the emotional complexities of growing up without a father, empowering you to move forward with clarity and strength.

Throughout the book, we have consistently suggested various forms of journaling as a therapeutic tool, and this is not by accident. Research has shown that regular journaling can significantly enhance emotional healing by helping you process complex feelings, track your progress, and gain deeper insight into your thoughts and emotions. Writing down your experiences and reflections helps to externalize and clarify emotions, making it easier to understand and work through them. By committing to journaling regularly, you create a space for ongoing self-reflection, which creates forward momentum in your healing journey. This consistent practice can be a powerful catalyst for change, helping you move past old emotional patterns and build a healthier, more resilient future.

Setting Personal Goals

Take a moment to consider what you hope to gain from engaging with this book. What are the specific areas of your life you wish to transform or understand more deeply? Write down a few personal goals for your journey through these pages, keeping them visible as a reminder of your intentions. As you progress, revisit these goals to assess your growth and adjust them as needed, allowing flexibility and room for new insights.

The process of healing is deeply personal and requires a commitment to self-discovery. This book is not a quick fix but a guide to help you manage the complexities of your emotions and experiences. It is written to offer support, understanding, and practical strategies that resonate with your unique journey. Through active engagement, you can transform the insights within these pages into tools for growth, empowerment, and healing.

Unique Journeys: Embracing Your Individual Path

The path to healing is as unique as your fingerprint, shaped by personal experiences and the nuances of your life journey. It's essential to recognize that healing is not a straight line. There will be days of progress and others where old wounds may resurface. It's okay to experience this ebb and flow. Your journey is yours alone, and it deserves to be honored as such. By acknowledging this, you allow yourself the grace to grow at your own pace, recognizing both your strengths and the areas where you have room to flourish. This understanding can be liberating, freeing you from the pressure to adhere to a rigid timeline or expectation.

In a world that often encourages comparison, it's easy to measure your progress against others. But healing is not a competition, and comparing your journey to someone else's can be detrimental. Celebrate your milestones, no matter how small they may seem. Each step forward, each moment of clarity or peace, is a testament to your resilience. Embrace these achievements and allow them to fuel your motivation. Avoid the trap of unrealistic standards, which can create unnecessary stress and self-doubt. Instead, set goals that are aligned with your personal values and aspirations, acknowledging that what works for one person might not work for another.

Embracing your individuality means tailoring your healing strategies to suit your personal preferences and needs. Only you know what resonates with your soul, what brings you comfort and peace. Whether it's engaging in art therapy, practicing mindfulness, or seeking support from a community group, choose the methods that speak to you. Create a personalized self-care plan that encompasses these practices, one that nurtures your mind, body, and spirit. This plan is a living document, evolving as you do, adapting to your changing needs and circumstances. By honoring your individuality, you empower yourself to heal in an authentic and sustainable way. The important thing is you must prioritize and commit to it; make time in your schedule the same way you would for a doctor's appointment.

Building confidence in self-directed healing is about trusting your intuition and instincts. You have a wealth of knowledge within you, drawn from past experiences and lessons learned. Reflect on decisions you have made and the insights these have provided. What have you discovered about yourself? What strengths have emerged in moments of adversity? Use this reflection as a foundation for setting intentions for future growth. Consider what you wish to explore, learn, or achieve in the coming months or years. These intentions are your inspiration and motivation to keep you grounded in your personal truth.

Reflection and Intention Setting

Find a quiet space to sit with a journal and reflect on your journey as a daughter who grew up without a father. Write down the milestones you've reached, the challenges you've overcome, and the strengths you've discovered along the way. Acknowledge how the legacy of trauma has shaped you, and recognize the courage it takes to move forward despite it. Next, set three intentions for your future growth, these could relate to personal development, relationships, or healing from past wounds. Keep this page as a reminder of your commitment to yourself and your continued journey toward healing.

As you work through this process, remember that there is no one right way to heal from the trauma of an absent father. Your journey is uniquely yours, and it deserves to be treated with patience and care. Trust in your ability to move through it at your own pace, knowing you have the strength to break free from the past. You have the power to create a future of healing, growth, and fulfillment.

Confronting Painful Memories with Care

Facing painful memories of growing up without a father can feel overwhelming, as if you're standing on the edge of a vast ocean, with emotions threatening to pull you under. However, acknowledging these memories is a vital step in healing. Unresolved trauma from the absence of a father can affect your present life in many ways, from shaping your sense of self-worth to influencing your relationships and decisions. It may show up as feelings of abandonment, difficulty trusting others, or even physical symptoms that reflect the emotional weight you've carried. For example, you might remember feeling intensely lonely during family events, birthdays, graduation ceremonies, sporting events, and school performances when other girls had their fathers there to support them and you did not. Perhaps you remember the extreme anxiety you felt when you were playing sports and looked at the sidelines to see all the other dads along the sidelines, supporting their daughters and no one there for you. Did you feel like an outcast, like you were inherently different from all the other kids because you didn't have a dad? Another painful memory might be that of having to rely on yourself for emotional support, even in times of distress, because your father wasn't there to provide comfort. When these memories are left unaddressed, they can hold you back, preventing you from fully embracing the present. Confronting them and working through them takes away their power over you and allows you to understand how they've shaped you, helping you gain the clarity needed for healing.

Approach these memories carefully, understanding that taking small steps is okay. Gradual exposure to these painful experiences in environments where you feel safe and supported can help you process them without feeling overwhelmed. You might choose a quiet, familiar space at home, or perhaps a therapist's office where you can get guidance and emotional support. Trusted friends who understand your history can also provide comfort and a listening ear. It's important to pace yourself and allow these memories to come up slowly, acknowledging them without letting them take over.

Reframing painful memories involves transforming them into something you can manage. Writing letters to your past self or your absent father figure can be a powerful way to release pent-up emotions. In these letters, express the feelings you couldn't share then. Be raw and honest, letting the words flow freely. This act allows you to externalize your emotions and make sense of them. Additionally, visualizing positive outcomes or lessons learned from these experiences can help shift your perspective. Picture yourself growing stronger, more resilient, and empowered because of what you've been through. This shift in perspective emphasizes growth rather than pain, helping you move from victimhood to empowerment.

Working through these memories builds emotional resilience and self-awareness. Reflecting on your growth as you work through the trauma of an absent father can be enlightening. Think about how you've changed, the strengths you've developed, and the obstacles you've overcome. These reflections can highlight your progress and remind you of your ability to handle future challenges. Practicing self-compassion is key in this process. Be kind to yourself, just as you would to a friend who has gone through similar experiences. Remember, revisiting these memories takes courage, and you deserve to treat yourself with patience and care.

Memory Mapping

Create a "memory map" to help visualize your journey and the impact of your father's absence. Start by drawing a horizontal line on a piece of paper to represent a timeline of your life. Mark significant events related to your father's absence along the timeline—this could include moments of emotional pain, feelings of abandonment, or specific memories of not having your father present. As you mark each event, note the emotions you associate with it, such as sadness, anger, or loneliness.

Once you've listed these events, take time to reflect on how they have influenced your present life. Are there recurring patterns, like difficulty trusting others or challenges with self-worth? Consider how these events shaped your views on relationships, your self-identity, and your emotional responses. In the space next to each event, write down any lessons learned or strengths gained as a result of these experiences.

For example, you may have developed resilience, independence, or the ability to seek support from others.

Use this memory map as a tool to understand your past and recognize the areas where you've grown. The map is a visual representation of your healing journey, helping you see how far you've come and how each experience has contributed to your growth. This map is also a reminder of your strength, showing you that despite the emotional challenges, you've built resilience and the capacity to heal.

By confronting these memories with clarity and compassion, you take back control of your narrative. You have the power to transform these painful moments into lessons that support your healing and future growth. The map becomes a foundation for understanding your past, empowering you to move forward with strength and self-awareness.

Moving Beyond Blame: Empowerment Through Action

Blame can feel like a heavy burden, one that offers a sense of certainty in the chaos that comes with being abandoned by a father. It settles over you, often becoming a way to direct the pain and anger you feel from the absence of a father figure. As a daughter, it's easy to internalize that abandonment and feel as though the absence is somehow your fault. You might ask yourself, "What did I do wrong? Why wasn't I enough to keep him around?" These thoughts can make blame feel like a protective shield, a way to rationalize the hurt and confusion, but it also prevents healing. Holding onto this blame keeps you stuck in the victim narrative, where the focus remains on what was lost, on the absence of your father, rather than what you can create moving forward.

Understanding that the blame you carry is misdirected is a crucial first step in your healing journey. While blaming your father may initially seem justified, it places the power to heal outside of yourself, relying on things that were beyond your control. Let me be very clear: the absence of your father is in no way connected to you or a reflection upon you. It is a reflection of him and all of his shortcomings, not yours. Your father's absence wasn't your fault, but holding onto that blame takes away your ability to move forward. Recognizing this allows you to reclaim your story, shifting the focus from what you didn't get to what you can now create for yourself.

Moving away from blame doesn't mean ignoring the pain or pretending that the hurt of abandonment didn't happen. It means choosing to take empowered steps toward healing, even if the circumstances of your upbringing weren't ideal. Begin by setting goals for personal growth, whether in your career, relationships, or self-discovery. Break these down into small, achievable steps that help you gain confidence and build momentum. As you take responsibility for your own healing, you begin to understand that while you couldn't control your father's absence, you do have the power to shape your future. This mindset allows you to move from being a passive participant in your life to actively creating the life you deserve.

True empowerment comes from taking intentional actions that build your confidence. Seek out experiences that challenge you, whether it's learning a new skill, exploring a new interest, or stepping into leadership roles. These actions remind you of your ability to overcome obstacles and grow. Self-advocacy is also key, being able to voice your needs and desires in relationships, at work, and in all areas of your life. Assertiveness is about expressing yourself with clarity and respect, reinforcing your worth and setting boundaries that protect your well-being. Each time you advocate for yourself, you reinforce your strength and create new opportunities for connection and growth.

Ultimately, moving beyond blame is about taking ownership of your life and embracing the possibility of transformation. It's about letting go of the past and stepping into a future where you define your own narrative. This process can be difficult, but each step forward is a testament to your resilience and capacity for growth. As you continue to work through your healing, know that you have the power to shape a future filled with strength, self-discovery, and fulfillment.

Moving Past the Anger

The absence of a father can leave daughters feeling a deep sense of abandonment and frustration, which often manifests as anger. This anger isn't always directed outwardly, but it simmers beneath the surface, making it hard to fully connect with others or trust the intentions of those around them. The hurt caused by not having a father present can make daughters feel as though they were somehow unworthy or undeserving of their father's love, leading to anger at the situation and themselves. The feeling of being rejected by someone who was supposed to provide unconditional love and protection can create a painful cycle of anger that becomes difficult to break.

This anger can take on many forms. Sometimes, it's a quiet, simmering frustration that appears in moments of vulnerability, when others around you talk about their fathers or when you experience milestones in life that would traditionally involve a father's support, such as graduation or a wedding. In these moments, the absence is felt more acutely, and the anger bubbles up, not necessarily because of what you've lost, but because of what others take for granted. Other times, this anger might manifest in outbursts or emotional distance in relationships, especially with men. It can create a fear of getting too close, a desire to protect yourself from potential abandonment, even when there's no reason to fear.

The frustration also often comes from the sense of not having control over what happened. As a child, you had no say in your father's absence, and this lack of control can fuel feelings of helplessness, which then turn into anger. You may feel as though you were forced into a situation that shaped your sense of self-worth and made it more difficult to trust others or feel truly loved. The resentment builds over time, especially if your father's absence was not openly discussed or acknowledged. It feels as though no one has truly recognized the depth of your pain, which only adds to the anger and disillusionment you carry.

In many cases, this anger also extends to the relationships that form after your father's absence. As a daughter without a father, you may find yourself searching for male figures to fill the emotional gap, but often these relationships are fraught with disappointment or disconnection. It's easy to project your anger onto other men, expecting them to fill the role your father never did, and when they inevitably fall short, the anger grows. This cycle of unmet expectations can be exhausting, and the constant questioning of whether anyone can truly be trusted can leave you emotionally drained.

Part of healing from this anger involves understanding that it is a normal reaction to a deep wound. The anger you feel is valid, it's a response to the emotional neglect and abandonment you've experienced. But holding onto that anger without processing it can continue to affect your emotional health and relationships. The first step is acknowledging the anger without shame or self-blame. It's important to give yourself permission to feel the hurt and frustration, but also to understand that healing requires releasing this anger so it doesn't continue to define your life.

Learning to move past this anger involves reframing your understanding of what you need from others and how you view yourself. Part of this process is coming to terms with the fact that your father's absence was not a reflection of your worth. You didn't cause his absence, and you are not defined by it. This reframing can be challenging, especially when so much of your life has been affected by the anger and hurt caused by this loss. But as you work through the layers of pain, you begin to realize that you have the power to heal, to reclaim your sense of worth, and to build healthier relationships based on trust and respect, not anger and fear.

Chapter 11

The absence of a father can leave a deep sense of isolation, making you feel disconnected from the world around you. Building a supportive community, a tribe, can change that. It starts with finding people who understand your history and trauma, those who have walked similar paths and can relate to your experiences.

Joining or starting a local support group or meetup can be incredibly helpful. These spaces allow for shared stories and mutual understanding. Whether through clubs or organizations with common goals, these connections provide more than just social interaction; they offer emotional support. The diverse perspectives in these groups can broaden your outlook and help you find new ways to approach challenges.

Identify Your Tribe

Take a moment to reflect on the kind of support network you wish to build. Consider the following:

- Who are the people that make you feel seen and understood?

- What shared interests or goals can bring you together?

- How can you contribute to creating a safe and nurturing

environment?

By exploring these questions, you begin to lay the foundation for your tribe, a community where your experiences are valued and your growth is supported.

Sharing Stories: The Power of Community

Sharing personal stories helps build connection and healing within a community. When you share your experience, you invite others to understand your world, creating empathy and validation. Hearing others' stories allows you to recognize common emotions and experiences, breaking down isolation and fostering unity.

To make this happen, create spaces for storytelling. Hosting events or workshops gives people a safe space to share their stories. You can also use online platforms like blogs or podcasts to reach a wider audience, allowing individuals to share their experiences authentically and connect with others. These spaces help reclaim narratives, turning past struggles into sources of strength.

Including diverse voices in storytelling enriches the community. Inviting speakers from different backgrounds expands perspectives and deepens understanding. Encouraging the sharing of cultural experiences leads to inclusivity and strengthens the sense of connection. Active listening is key to making these stories powerful; by truly listening and providing empathetic feedback, you validate the speaker's emotions and create a space where stories are not only heard but felt.

Engaging with Online Support Networks

Online support networks offer a valuable space for daughters who grew up without their fathers to connect with others who share similar experiences. These platforms break down geographical barriers, creating a space to engage with people who understand your pain. Whether through online forums, support groups, or social media communities, these virtual spaces provide connection, empathy, and healing. In these communities, shared experiences bind individuals, offering a sense of belonging and understanding that may have been missing in your offline life.

There are many benefits to engaging with online support networks. You can participate from the comfort of your home, engaging on your own terms and at your own pace. This accessibility ensures that support is always available, whether you're seeking advice, sharing your own story, or finding reassurance in knowing you're not alone. Additionally, the global nature of these networks exposes you to diverse perspectives, helping you understand your own experiences in new ways. Online engagement can also be a powerful catalyst for personal growth, providing a supportive environment to explore and heal.

However, it's important to approach these spaces with mindfulness, particularly regarding privacy and safety. Setting clear boundaries about what you're comfortable sharing and what you wish to keep private ensures that your online experiences remain positive and secure. Engaging in respectful, empathetic conversations can help build meaningful connections with others. Reaching out to individuals with similar experiences can lead to lasting friendships and a sense of community, both online and offline, that can provide support and encouragement.

Long-Term Healing: Sustaining Growth and Change

Healing is an ongoing process that requires continuous attention and care. Personal growth doesn't stop after initial progress, especially for daughters who grew up without a father. It takes commitment to keep evolving. Setting regular goals for personal development is necessary to staying focused and moving forward. These goals act as railings, helping you align your actions with the person you want to become. Reflecting on your progress, while acknowledging areas for further work, ensures that you stay true to your values and aspirations.

As you continue your growth, it's important to integrate practical strategies into your daily life. Regularly reassessing your action plans and adjusting them helps you stay on track. This might involve embracing new challenges or stepping out of your comfort zone. Learning through books, courses, or life experiences keeps you constantly gaining new insights that support your journey. Additionally, attending lectures or taking psychology classes at a local college can provide deeper understanding and tools for processing your past trauma. Embracing these opportunities for education can further empower your personal growth and healing.

It's essential to remember that healing doesn't follow a straight path. Unexpected triggers, whether situations or people, will inevitably bring past pain to the surface. This is a normal part of the healing process, and you should expect it. Having support in place, like a therapist, can help you manage these triggers. A therapist can provide a safe space for processing your childhood trauma and give you tools to cope when these emotions resurface. Therapy, combined with your personal efforts, ensures you stay on track and continue to make progress, even when past pain emerges unexpectedly.

Embracing Empathy and Understanding

For daughters who grew up without a father, empathy can be especially cathartic in healing the wounds of abandonment. When you've felt unseen or unsupported by your father, receiving empathy from others can create the connection you've longed for. It's like the warmth of a shared glance, the simple acknowledgment that someone understands your pain. Empathy allows you to feel seen and heard, validating your emotions and experiences. This validation is imperative for healing, as it helps to break the isolation that often comes with growing up without a father. By practicing empathy in relationships, you can build the trust and emotional safety needed to heal from childhood trauma and form stronger, supportive connections with others.

Practicing empathy starts with actively listening, truly engaging with the feelings of those around you. This means setting aside distractions and giving someone your full attention, making them feel understood. For daughters who have experienced their father's absence, this could mean seeking out those who truly listen, whether a trusted friend, therapist, or support group member. By asking open-ended questions and inviting deeper conversations, you create space for others to express their emotions, which in turn helps you do the same. Through these empathetic exchanges, you allow yourself to connect with others on a deeper level, helping to heal the emotional gaps left by your father's absence.

However, barriers to empathy can exist, particularly if you've internalized feelings of abandonment or mistrust. Many daughters without fathers may have hesitations about trusting others, stemming from past hurt. Overcoming these barriers involves challenging those old beliefs and allowing yourself to be open to receiving empathy. It requires patience with yourself and others, learning to embrace vulnerability and letting go of the fear of being hurt again. As you practice empathy, you begin to understand that it's not just about connecting with others, it's also about reconnecting with yourself. Each moment of empathy can help you heal, teaching you the importance of self-compassion and understanding.

Empathy ultimately becomes a tool for self-discovery. As you reflect on your own interactions, you begin to recognize how your past trauma has shaped your reactions, biases, and assumptions. This self-awareness allows you to grow emotionally, leading to greater emotional intelligence. By practicing empathy, you create a cycle of healing, not just for others, but for yourself as well. Each empathetic connection deepens your understanding of your own needs and emotions, helping you move forward with a greater sense of peace and acceptance.

Legacy of Healing: Passing It Forward

Healing from childhood trauma, especially for daughters whose fathers abandoned them, creates a ripple effect that extends beyond your personal journey. As you work through the pain and embrace growth, you transform your own life and become an inspiration for others. Your healing demonstrates that change is possible, offering others who've faced similar challenges the encouragement to continue their own path toward recovery. This process allows you to build a legacy of resilience, showing future generations that strength can emerge from adversity.

Mentoring others who have experienced similar trauma can be a powerful way to share this legacy. By offering guidance and support, you help others through their struggles, giving them direction and hope. Whether through writing, speaking, or leading support groups, your story can reach those who need it most, providing comfort and inspiration. These actions, sharing your story and supporting others, create a ripple effect, touching lives and creating a broader community of healing.

As you continue your healing, it's important to celebrate how your growth positively impacts those around you. Each step forward is a sign of your resilience and determination, and by acknowledging this, you inspire others to pursue their own healing. The legacy you create is not just about personal change; it's about empowering others and supporting a compassionate, understanding community. Your story becomes a source of strength, offering others the hope that they, too, can overcome their pain and build a better future.

Conclusion

Growing up without a father creates childhood trauma, which leaves deep emotional scars, feelings of abandonment, neglect, and confusion that can shape how you view yourself and the world. These struggles often involve difficulty trusting others, especially men, and feelings of inadequacy or unworthiness. The absence of a father figure can make it hard to form secure attachments, leading to challenges in relationships, self-esteem, and emotional regulation. You might have spent much of your life feeling unseen, unsupported, or as if you were never quite enough. These are painful realities, but they do not define you or limit your potential. As you work through this trauma, remember that a brighter, happier future is possible and within your reach.

Healing from this trauma isn't easy, and the process isn't linear. There will be setbacks, moments of doubt, and times when the pain feels overwhelming. But with every step you take towards healing, you are making progress. This journey requires patience, self-compassion, and the willingness to face your pain instead of avoiding it. It's about learning to manage the intense emotions tied to your father's absence, anger, sadness, grief, and using those emotions as tools for growth. Through techniques like mindfulness, journaling, and cognitive-behavioral strategies, you can begin to regulate your emotional responses and shift from a mindset of victimhood to one of empowerment. These practices help you understand that while your father's absence caused deep wounds, it does not determine the course of your life. You have the power to heal, rebuild, and reclaim your narrative.

A critical part of healing is building a support system. Daughters of absent fathers often feel isolated, carrying the weight of their pain without sharing it with others. But you don't have to go through this alone. Connecting with others who share similar experiences can provide much-needed validation and empathy. Whether through online communities, local support groups, or close friends who understand your struggles, these connections remind you that you are not alone. They also provide perspective, advice, and encouragement, helping you to heal by sharing your journey with others who truly understand.

It's also important to engage in your personal growth. While your past may have shaped you, it doesn't define who you are or who you can become. Explore your passions, set goals, and step outside your comfort zone to build confidence and self-worth. Each new experience or challenge is an opportunity to prove to yourself that you are capable of moving forward, no matter the obstacles. Whether you decide to take a class, pick up a new hobby, or go back to school to study something new, these efforts contribute to healing by allowing you to redefine yourself beyond the pain of the past.

Remember, healing doesn't mean erasing the past, but learning to live with it in a way that allows you to thrive. Acknowledge that the absence of your father created wounds that take time to heal, but it doesn't mean you are broken or unworthy. You can take back control of your story, shape a future that aligns with your values, and create a life full of joy, purpose, and fulfillment. The legacy of your father's absence doesn't have to be one of pain and brokenness, it can be a story of resilience, strength, and personal growth.

Your story is uniquely yours, and it's important to recognize the progress you make along the way. Healing is not about perfection, but about the courage to move forward, step by step. You have already proven your strength by facing the pain, and you will continue to grow and flourish as you release the past and step into the future. You have the power to heal, to rise above the legacy of abandonment, and to create a life that is rich with love, peace, and personal fulfillment. Keep moving forward, keep reaching for your dreams, and remember that you are worthy of everything that is yet to come.

References

References

BetterHelp. (n.d.). *Healing through storytelling: How stories can help you process trauma*. Retrieved from https://www.betterhelp.com/advice/research/healing-through-storytelling-how-narratives-can-help-you-process-trauma/

Choosing Therapy. (n.d.). *Childhood emotional neglect: Signs, effects, & how to heal*. Retrieved from https://www.choosingtherapy.com/childhood-emotional-neglect/

Choosing Therapy. (n.d.). *How to heal childhood trauma: 13 tips from a therapist*. Retrieved from https://www.choosingtherapy.com/healing-from-childhood-trauma/

Culture and Personal Identity. (n.d.). *National Center for Cultural Competence*. Georgetown University. Retrieved from https://nccc.georgetown.edu/curricula/awareness/C13.html

Emerge Healing Center. (n.d.). *Childhood trauma and toxic relationships*. Retrieved from https://emergehealingcenter.com/childhood-trauma-toxic-relationships/

Fatherless Daughters. (n.d.). *The impact of absence*. Psychology Today. Retrieved from https://www.psychologytoday.com/us/blog/transcending-the-past/202305/fatherless-daughters-the-impact-of-absence

Fatherless Daughter: About Us. (n.d.). *A Fatherless Daughter*. Retrieved from https://www.afatherlessdaughter.org/

Fatherless Daughter Syndrome: The Effects of an Absent Father. (n.d.). *Beat Anxiety*. Retrieved from https://beatanxiety.me/fatherless-daughter-syndrome-psycho logical-effects-of-an-absent-father-on-a-girl/

Father Wound: Signs in Daughters, Women and Men - AP. (n.d.). *The Attachment Project*. Retrieved from https://www.attachmentpr oject.com/psychology/father-wound/

Healthline. (n.d.). *How to use mindfulness to ease and heal trauma*. Retrieved from https://www.healthline.com/health/how-trauma-informed-mindful ness-helps-me-heal-from-the-past-and-cope-with-the-present

How Therapy for Childhood Trauma Can Help. (n.d.). *Healthline*. Retrieved from https://www.healthline.com/health/mental-he alth/therapy-for-childhood-trauma

How to Heal from a "Father-Wound". (2021, March 24). *Psychology Today*. Retrieved from https://www.psychologytoday.com/us/blog /the-forgiving-life/202103/how-to-heal-from-a-father-wound

How to Heal from Childhood Trauma: 3 Steps to Start Coping. (n.d.). *BetterUp*. Retrieved from https://www.betterup.com/blog/c hildhood-trauma

How to Overcome Perfectionism: 15 Worksheets & Strategies. (n .d.). *Positive Psychology*. Retrieved from https://positivepsychology.c om/how-to-overcome-perfectionism/

How to Use Mindfulness to Ease and Heal Trauma. (n.d.). *Healthline*. Retrieved from https://www.healthline.com/health/how-trauma-informed-mindful ness-helps-me-heal-from-the-past-and-cope-with-the-present

Perfectionism and Self-Sabotage: The Trap of Trying to Earn Parents' Love. (2021, November 16). *Intuitive Healing NYC*. Retrieved from https://www.intuitivehealingnyc.com/blog/2021/11/16/perfectionism-and-self-sabotage-the-trap-of-trying-to-earn-parents-love

Single Mother Parenting and Adolescent Psychopathology. (2017). *PubMed Central (PMC)*. Retrieved from https://pmc.ncbi.nlm.nih.gov/articles/PMC5226056/#:~:text=Girls%20were%20more%20susceptible%20to,prevalence%20of%20adolescent%20externalizing%20disorders

Support Groups: Make Connections, Get Help. (n.d.). *Mayo Clinic*. Retrieved from https://www.mayoclinic.org/healthy-lifestyle/stress-management/in-depth/support-groups/art-20044655

The Benefits of Emotional Vulnerability - Mental Health. (n.d.). *Framework Recovery*. Retrieved from https://frameworkrecovery.com/the-benefits-of-emotional-vulnerability/

The Healing Benefits of Journaling. (n.d.). *Mind Spirit Center*. Retrieved from https://mindspiritcenter.org/journaling/

The Lived Experience of Daughters Who Have Absent Fathers. (n.d.). *Walden University ScholarWorks*. Retrieved from https://scholarworks.waldenu.edu/cgi/viewcontent.cgi?article=5995&context=dissertations

The Power of Art Therapy: Unlocking Mental Wellness Through Creative Expression. (n.d.). *Anxiety Institute*. Retrieved from https://anxietyinstitute.com/the-power-of-art-therapy-unlocking-mental-wellness-through-creative-expression/

The Profound Effects of an Absent Father on Daughters. (n.d.). *Osita Ibekwe*. Retrieved from https://ositaibekwe.com/effects-of-an-absent-father-on-daughters/

The Use of Reauthoring and Therapeutic Letters. (n.d.). *Good Therapy*. Retrieved from https://www.goodtherapy.org/blog/narrative-therapy-reauthoring/

Trauma-Informed Mindfulness: A Guide. (n.d.). *Psych Central*. Retrieved from https://psychcentral.com/health/trauma-informed-mindfulness

Trust Issues: Rebuilding Trust After Childhood Trauma. (n.d.). *MHC Counseling Group*. Retrieved from https://mhcounselinggroup.com/mhc-mental-health-therapy-blog/trust-issues-rebuilding-trust-after-childhood-trauma

Understanding Trauma Healing Work: Empowering Survivors and Restoring Well-Being. (n.d.). *World Impact*. Retrieved from https://www.worldimpact.org/blog/understanding-trauma-healing-work-empowering-survivors-and-restoring-well-being/

Understanding and Overcoming Your Identity Crisis. (n.d.). *Taju Coaching*. Retrieved from https://www.tajucoaching.com/blog/navigating-maze-understanding-and-overcoming-identity-crisis

Why Self-Help Books Don't Work (And How to Benefit from Them). (2019, July 5). *Forbes*. Retrieved from https://www.forbes.com/sites/jeroenkraaijenbrink/2019/07/05/why-self-help-books-dont-work-and-how-to-nevertheless-benefit-from-them/

www.ingramcontent.com/pod-product-compliance
Ingram Content Group UK Ltd.
Pitfield, Milton Keynes, MK11 3LW, UK
UKHW020941140525
5909UKWH00019B/135